Spices, Condiments, Teas, Coffees and Other Delicacies

Roland Robertson

Spices, Condiments, Teas, Coffees and Other Delicacies

A GUIDE TO THE HARD TO FIND

Roland Robertson

OLIVER PRESS
WILLITS, CALIFORNIA

CHARLES SCRIBNER'S SONS
NEW YORK

First Printing January 1975

OLIVER PRESS
1400 Ryan Creek Road
Willits, California 95490

CHARLES SCRIBNER'S SONS
New York

CONTENTS

INTRODUCTION

In the search for gastronomic tantalization, one often finds the corner market somewhat lacking in inspiration. One then either goes home unsatisfied or, if living in, say, New York, fights traffic and drives until finding a gourmet store that carries the item desired. This book is an attempt to alleviate that situation.

Like to have some pickled pig's knuckles, or some beluga caviar? Look in the index under whatever delicacy strikes your fancy and there, under the food, is a list of companies from which the tasty morsel can be obtained. Look up the listed companies in the Company Index and there is a description of the company, a list of their other products, and information about their catalog.

We have tried to include as many companies as possible, with the only requirements being that they have a catalog and sell by mail order. It is hoped that subsequent revisions of this guide will remedy such unintentional errors or omissions as might have occurred and that frequent revisions will keep the guide abreast of the world of spices, teas and other exotica.

This guide consists of two main indexes: a MASTER INDEX and a COMPANY INDEX. The MASTER INDEX is a list of products alphabetically arranged. If you are looking for a specific product, first check for it in the MASTER INDEX. The MASTER INDEX will tell you which company or companies offer the specific product.

MASTER INDEX

Roth and Sons
COCOA almonds
    Paprikas Weiss Importer
COCOA flavoring
    Paprikas Weiss Importer
COCONUT
    Kalustyan
COCONUT, cream of
    Kam Shing Co.
COCONUT flavoring
    Paprikas Weiss Importer
COCONUT oil
    Sahadi Import Co.
COCONUT patties
    The Swiss Colony

Next check the COMPANY INDEX to find out more about each company listed. The COMPANY INDEX offers information about each company, the range of its products, as well as details about its catalog. If the description of a company sounds interesting, by all means write to the company directly. Only the company itself can provide final, authoritative information about its products and prices. Don't hesitate to write to more than one company if more than one company provides the specific product in which you are interested. In this way you can compare before you buy.

COMPANY INDEX

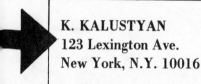

K. KALUSTYAN
123 Lexington Ave.
New York, N.Y. 10016

PRODUCTS:

Agarbatti
Bombay duck
Chillies
Chutney
Coconut
Dalls

Flour:
   graham
   rice
    wheat
Mint
Pickles
Rice
Varian

An unusual selection of foodstuffs—Armenian, Indian, Pakistani, Turkish, Iranian. Whether one's taste runs to Basmatti rice, Agarbatti or garlic chutney, this is the place.

Catalog 25¢ with pre-addressed envelope

COMPANY INDEX

ALL ORGANICS, INC.
15870 S.W. 216th St.
Miami, Fla. 33170

PRODUCTS:

   Avocados   Mangos

This company offers tropical fruits and winter vegetables, their specialties being Mangos from July through August and Avacados available from July through December. Folks in colder climates can be glad for the mild Florida winters which allow such goodies to be enjoyed on snowy December days.

Catalog is free

AMANA SOCIETY
Meat Dept.
Amana, Iowa 52203

PRODUCTS:

Bacon, smoked
Canadian Bacon
Cervelat
Cheese, cheddar
Cheese products
Sausage sticks

Amana smoked meat specialties, a gourmet's delight from the famed Amana Colonies in Iowa since 1854, are ready to give your dinner guests the same treat people have been enjoying for over 100 years. Their cheddar cheese and cheese spread are not to be taken lightly as they are produced under the same high standards as Amana's smoked hams, bacon and sausage. They specialize in meat and cheese gift boxes with prices ranging from around $7.00 for the sausage twin pack to approaching $40.00 for a super deluxe package of whole hams, bacon and sausage.

Price list is free

APHRODISIA
28 Carmine St.
New York, N.Y. 10014

PRODUCTS:

Absinthe
Adam & Eve root
Agar agar
Agrimony
Aloe
Althea root
Alfalfa
Alma seeds

2

Allspice

Ambrette seeds

Angelica root

Annatto seeds

Arabic, gum

Arnica flowers

Anise

Arrowroot

Asifoetida

Balm of Gilead

Basil

Bayberry bark

Bay leaves

Benzoin

Berberi

Betel nuts

Birch bark

Bistort

Black beans

Blackberry leaves

Black Cohosh

Black Haw bark

Black Willow bark

Bladderwrack

Blueberry leaves

Blue cohosh

Boldo

Boneset

Borage

Bouquet garni

Buchu leaves

Buckeyes

Buckthorne bark

Burdock root

Cactus flowers

Calamus root

Caraway seeds

Cardamon

Cassia bark

Catnip

Cayenne pepper

Cedar powder

Celery flakes

Celery seeds

Centuary herb

Chamomile

Chaparral

Chervil

Cherries, dried

Cherry seeds

Cherry stems

Chickweed

Chili peppers

Chili powder

Chives

Chrysanthemum flowers

Cinnamon

Clover blossoms, red

Cloves

Cola nuts

Coltsfoot

Comfrey

Corn flowers

Coriander

Cubeb berries

Curry powder

Cumin seed

Daisy flowers

Damiana

Dandelion

Deers Tongue

Dill

Dittany of Crete

Dong Quai (Korean)

Dragon's Blood powder

Echinacea

Elder flowers

Elecampne

Epazote

Euphorbia herb

Eyebright

Fennel seeds

Fenugreek seed

Five Finger Grass

Flax seeds

Fleabane

Fo Ti Teng

Galangal

Garlic

Gentian

Ginger

Ginseng

Goldenseal

Gotu cola

Grains of Paradise

Green peppercorns

Guaram Masala

Guiacum chips

Guarana

Hawthorne berries

Heal All

Heliotropin

Henna

Hi John the Conqueror root

Hibiscus flowers

Hyssop

Honeysuckle flowers

Horsetail

Horehound

Hops

Huckleberries

Irish Moss

Jaborandi leaves

Jericho (Ressurection) Flower

Jewelweed

Juniper berries

Kelp

Lady's Mantle

Lady's Slipper

Leeks

Lemongrass

Lemon peel

Lemon Verbena

Licorice root

Life Everlasting

Lily buds

Lilacs, crystallized

Lili of the Valley leaves

Linden tea

Lobelia

Lotus

Lovage root

Lucky Hand (Salap root)

Mace

Mahlab

Maidenhair

Malva flowers

Marigold flowers

Marjoram

Mastic

Mimosa

Marshmallow root

Mint leaves

Mistletoe

Mugwort

Motherwort

Mu Tea

Mullien

Mushrooms

Mustard seeds, black

Mustard seeds, yellow

Mustard powder

Myrrh

Musk, crystals

Musk root

Nettle

Nutmeg

Oak Moss

Orange blossoms

Orange peel

Onions, chopped

Onions, powder

Oregano

Orris root

Passion Flower

Papaya leaves

Parsley

Paprika

Paraguay Tea

Patchouli leaves

Peach leaves

Peach seeds

Pennyroyal

Peppercorns

Peppermint

Periwinkle

Pickling spice

Pignoli (Pine Nuts)

Pipsissewa

Plantain

Peony root

Pleurisy Root

Poke Root

Pomander

Pomegranate seeds

Poppy flowers

Poppy seeds

Primrose

Psyllium seeds

Queen of the Meadow

Quassia chips

Quinine bark

Raspberries, dried

Red Raspberry leaves

Rock candy

Rosebuds

Rosemary

Roses, crystallized

Rosewater, French

Rosewood powder

Rue

Safflower

Saffron

Sage

Sarsaparilla root

St. John's Wort

Salt

Sandalwood

Savory

Saw Palmetto berries

Senna pods

Senna leaves

Sassafras

Shallots

Sesame seeds

Sesame oil

Sesame Tahine

Skullcap

Slippery Elm bark

Sourwood leaves

Soursalt

Southern John the Conqueror root

Southernwood

Solomon's Seal

Spearmint

Spikenard

Strawberry leaves

Sumac

Sunflowers

Supare (Mangalore)

Szechuan pepper

Tag Alder bark

Tamarind

Tangerine peel

Tansy

Tarragon

Thyme

Tragacanth gum

Tiger Balm

Tonka beans

Turmeric

Valerian root

Vanilla beans

Vanillin

Uva Ursi

Vegetable flakes

Vervain

Vetivert

Violet leaves

Violets, crystallized

Wahoo bark

Walnut leaves.

Water Eryngo root

Watermelon seeds

Water Pepper

White Ash bark

White Oak bark

White Willow bark

Wild Alum root

Wild Cherry bark

Wild Yam root

Wintergreen

Witchhazel

Wood Betony

Woodruff

Wormseed

Yarrow

Yellow Dock

Yerba Mate

Yerba Santa

Zebrovka

One of the most extensive offerings of exotic herbs, spices, condiments and essential oils available. The people at Aphrodisia have amassed a huge volume of information, as their interesting and informative catalog will show, and they not only have a nearly complete list of herbs and spices to sell, but also give you the facts and folklore as well as recipes. Of special interest is a large (30x40) herbal study chart with herb and ailment cross-referencing.

Catalog is free

THE APPLEYARD CORPORATION
Maple Corner
Calais, Vt. 05648

PRODUCTS:

Cereals, mixed	Jelly, apple cider
Cheese, Vermont Colby	Syrup, maple
Chutney	Tomato products

A smaller company, they produce such goodies as chutney and tomato conserve by hand, using no synthetic compounds or additives. They even cut up the nuts, raisins, apricots and sunflower seeds in their Cornucopia mixed cereal by hand to give a random size to the pieces (unobtainable any other way). Their Crowley Vermont Cheese is also made the slow, careful way, with nothing added. They have an adequate but limited supply of cheese and a goodly pantry of 100% natural Maple Syrup. The concern and personal attention given each order insures quality and service.

Price list sent free of charge

BACCHANALIA
273 Riverside Ave.
Westport, Conn. 06880

PRODUCTS:

Beer/wine making supplies	Flavorings/extracts, soft drink
	Fruit, dried

BACCHANALIA (Cont'd)

Bacchus himself would surely approve of this list of ingredients, supplies and equipment for making wine, beer, liquers and other potables. Everything needed by the experienced winemaker to prepare and bottle his favorite drink as well as kits for the beginner are included in Bacchanalia's list of products.

12 page catalog is free

BAILEY'S OF BOSTON, INC.
26 Temple Place
Boston, Mass. 02111

Candy:
    bon-bons
    caramel
    hard
    jelly
    mint
Chocolate, filled
Fruit cake
Fudge
Nuts
Peanuts, salted
Pecans
Toppings, dessert

Hand-made candies from recipes developed over the past 100 years have given Bailey's a world-wide reputation for quality, service and integrity. Their dark and milk chocolates come in a variety of flavors and fillings, including creams, caramels, nuts and fruits. They also carry imported filled tins, fruit cake, and a moderate list of nuts. Bailey's maintains lists of their customers' personal selections for future reference as many leave standing orders for personal mixtures to be sent

8

BAILEY'S OF BOSTON, INC (Cont'd)

automatically to friends at periodic intervals. Bailey's also guarantees each shipment.

Price list free of charge

BERNARD FOOD INDUSTRIES, INC.
222 S. 24th St.
San Jose, Calif. 95103

PRODUCTS:

Camping/storage foods

Bernard's Kamp Pack line was developed to meet the needs of outdoorsmen, scouts, hunters and campers. A large variety of selections plus high nutritional value makes out-of-doors living a little more convenient:

Price list is free

BISSINGER'S
205 W. 4th St.
Cincinnati, Ohio

PRODUCTS:

Biscuits, sweet/shortbread
Caviar
Chocolate:
   filled
   milk
Cocktail mixes
Crackers, oriental
Fruit, mixed fresh
Grapefruit
Steak

BISSINGER'S (Cont'd)

Although mainly in the boxed chocolate business, Bissinger's also carries such gourmet items as caviar, English shortbreads, and gift packages of steaks and fruits. Through their affiliation with the world-wide Telefood organization, they can deliver baskets of even the most perishable fruits on 24 hour notice to most places in the United States and many places abroad.

16 page illustrated catalog free

BOGGIATTO PACKING CO., INC.
11000 Blackie Rd., Dept. OP
Castroville, Calif. 95012

PRODUCTS:

Artichokes/artichoke hearts

From Castroville, California, the artichoke capital of the world, come Boggiatto's "Mr. Artichoke" brand artichokes. They also feature a line of winter artichokes; bronze leaves, frost flavored. These gourmet delights can be ordered in boxes of 24 small artichokes or 12 large ones. They also include their booklet "Artichokes are Fun to Eat" free with every order. It tells the story of artichokes and contains many delicious recipes.

Price list free

BREAKFAST CREEK FARM
P.O. Box 429
Prattville, Ala. 36067

PRODUCTS:

Fudge
Pecans/pecan products

Breakfast Creek Farm, built 150 years ago, is surrounded by 212 acres of pecan trees and pine forest. Their large, Stuart variety pecans can be ordered as roasted halves, unroasted halves, or in the shell, as well as covered with a light glace confection. Pecans are shipped seasonally with orders going out usually starting no later than November 12th.

Illustrated price list free

BREMAN HOUSE, INC.
200 E. 86th St.
New York, N.Y. 10028

PRODUCTS:

Artichokes/artichoke hearts
Asparagus
Bouillon/soup flavorings
Breads, European
Bread, pumpernickle
Bread, rye
Candy, imported
Cheese, exotic imported

Cheese:

  France
  Germany
  Holland
  Switzerland

BREMEN HOUSE, INC. (Cont'd)

Cocoa
Coffee, decaffienated
Coffee, imported
Confections, European
Cookies, imported
Crackers/wafers, European
Fish, freshwater
Flavoring essences
Flours/mixes, European
Ginseng/ginseng products
Hearts of Palm
Herring/herring products
Honey, imported
Kraut
Lobster/lobster products
Marzipan
Meat products, European style
Meat specialties, imported

Mushrooms
Pickles, German
Potato products
Poultry/game products
Preserves, imported fruit
Puddings/pudding mixes
Salmon/salmon products
Seafood, imported
Seasonings/sauces
Shrimp/shrimp products
Spices
Syrups, imported fruit
Tea, English
Tea, herb
Tonics
Vegetables, imported
Wurst

Breman House offers gourmet specialties from all over the world. While concentrating on German and East European style foods, they also have such delicacies as Scottish game products, cheeses from France, Holland and Denmark, and fine English teas. They don't stop here either. Their long list of herbs for health and refreshment features many rare and unusual varieties. In addition to their food products, Breman House carries a line of European utensils, colognes, magazines, newspapers and phonograph records.

BUTTERFIELD FARMS, INC.
8500 Wilshire Blvd., Suite 1005
Beverly Hills, Calif. 90211

PRODUCTS:

Fruitcake

Although they offer only one product, fruitcake, Butterfield
Farms calls it "The World's Most Expensively Made Fruitcake," and it may well be. Using walnuts from France, raisins
from California, Malaysian pineapple, Spanish almonds and
pecans from the south, Butterfield Farms puts it all together
and adds 100 proof, aged in the wood, bonded Kentucky
bourbon, 86 proof New England rum and 80 proof brandy
to make a true fruitcake lover's treat.

Colorful brochure and price list free

BYRD COOKIE CO.
P.O. Box 13086
Savannah, Ga. 31406

PRODUCTS:

Candy, benne
Cakes, rice
Cocktail bits, cheese
Cocktail bits, onion/garlic
Cookies, cream filled
Crackers/wafers, seed

Step back into history with the Byrd Cookie Company and
discover an authentic turn of the century cookie shanty.
Founded in 1924 in the Old Fort section of Savannah, Georgia,
the Byrd Cookie Company has stayed around and continues
to make such goodies as Benne candy, cocktail bits, cream
filled cookies and benne wafers. Benne is a seed which was
originally brought to the coastal areas of Georgia and South
Carolina by the early slaves. Planted near the slave quarters,

13

BYRD COOKIE CO. (Cont'd)

benne became a traditional part of the Old South and many
recipes for exotic concoctions have passed down to allow
Byrd Cookie Company to produce their line of candies,
cookies and crackers. Not one to rest on their laurels, they
use hard-to-get wild rice in their rice tea cakes and send them
on to customers with a guarantee of perfect delivery.

Price list free

CARAVEL COFFEE CO.
P.O. Box 554
Jackson Heights, N.Y. 11372

PRODUCTS:

Coffee blends
Darjeeling
Tea, black
Tea, blends
Tea, green

Caravel sells high quality coffee and teas and several interesting coffee blends. The company, upon request, will gift wrap
and include a gift card at no extra cost.

Brochure free

CAROB PRODUCTS
P.O. Box 5084
Walnut Creek, Calif. 94596

PRODUCTS:

Carob/carob products

The carob is a pod which grows on a tree of the locust family.
A good supply of these carob trees grow in Southern California and Baja California, Mexico. From these pods is manu-

CAROB PRODUCTS (Cont'd)

factured a flour used to make a variety of candies, cookies, breads, pastries and more. The fruit of the carob tree, often known as St. John's Bread, is often used as a healthful substitute for chocolate and is noted for its natural sweetness and flavoring. Carob Products sells molasses from the Mediterranean, carob spread, flour, syrup and natural pods.

Descriptive brochure free, catalog in the making

CATHERINE'S CHOCOLATE SHOP
Cooper Rd.
Great Barrington, Mass. 01230

PRODUCTS:

Chocolate, filled
Dietetic products
Nuts
Peanut brittle

For years, people who know good chocolate have acclaimed Catherine's. All are hand made and dipped by master New England confectioners from tradition-tested recipes. For some items, the customer can choose between bittersweet, milk or white chocolate. For a unique treat Catherine's offers a package of chocolate covered pretzels. Now there's something you don't often find in your neighborhood grocery.

Illustrated brochure and price list free

CELESTIAL SEASONINGS
P.O. Box 1405
Boulder, Colo. 80302

PRODUCTS:

Ginseng/ginseng products
Herbs, aromatic
Tea, herb

A rapidly growing herb tea company with a large line of herbs and herb teas, Celestial Seasonings takes care that their plants are not sprayed or chemically fertilized, and are as nutritionally valuable as possible. They feature blends, singles, tea bags and tableted herbs. For example, their Red Zinger blend contains rose hips, hibiscus flowers, lemon grass, wintergreen, lemon peel, peppermint and wild cherry bark. They also carry forty different single herbs, from alfalfa to yarrow, from which the customer can create his own blends. Within the coming year, Celestial Seasonings will be contracting organic herb crops all over the world as well as growing their own on 1,000 acres, and plan soon to have a complete line of quality herbs.

Descriptive brochure free

R. H. CHAMBERLIN
  Gift Fruit Shipper
1940 Barr St.
Merritt Island, Fla. 32952

PRODUCTS:

Crabs/crab products
Grapefruit, fresh
Key lime pies
Lobsters/lobster products
Murcotts
Oranges, navel
Oranges, temple

Oranges, Valencia	Snapper
Shrimp/shrimp products	Tangelos

Indian River citrus fruit from Florida is often considered the best in the world. This company offers a wide variety of oranges, grapefruit and some of the newer citrus fruits. In addition, some deep water Florida seafood is sold. Ordering from their catalog might even make a Florida vacation unnecessary.

12 page color catalog 25¢

CHARLOTTE CHARLES, INC.
2542 N. Elston Ave.
Chicago, Ill. 60647

PRODUCTS:

BREADS, CRACKERS, FLOUR MIXES

Bread, brown
Bread, pumpernickel
Crackers/wafers, oriental
Crackers/wafers, seed
Crepes/crepe mixes
Dumplings/dumpling mixes
Pancake mixes
Toasts/crispbreads

CAKES, COOKIES, SHELLS

Biscuits, sweet/shortbreads
Bouchees
Cakes, rum
Cookies:

ginger	orange
lemon	vanilla

Cookies:

    chocolate chip

    ginger

    lemon

    orange

    vanilla

Fortune cookies

Fruit and nut bars

Fruit cake

Nut loaves

Petit fours

Pie/pastry shells

Pralines

Puffs

CANDIES, CHOCOLATES

Candy:

    bonbons

    caramel

    French

    fruit

    mint

Chocolate, Swiss

Marzipan

Toffees

CAVIAR, SEAFOODS

Anchovies

Caviar:

    Beluga

    Danish lumpfish

    salmon

Clams/clam products

Crabs/crab products

Herring/herring products

Kipper snacks

Mussels

Octopus

Oysters/oyster products

Salmon/salmon products

Sardines/sardine products

Shrimp/shrimp products

Snails

Squid

Tuna/tuna products

CEREALS, COCKTAIL SNACKS

Cereals, dry

Cocktail bits, corn

Oatmeal

Sunflower seeds

COFFEES, TEAS, COCOA

Cocoa

Coffee, Hawaiian

Tea, English

Tea, Formosa

FRUITS, NUTS

Apple rings

Apple sauce

Apricots

Cherries, maraschino

Coconuts/coconut products

Crabapples

Figs

Fruits in liquers

Fruits, salad

Grapefruit segments

Melons, sweet pickled

Nuts

Olives

Orange segments

Peaches, prepared

Pecans/pecan products

Pineapple

Plums, prepared

Prunes

JUICES

Juice:

apple

apricot

grapefruit

pineapple

vegetable

MEATS, PREPARED MEALS

Chili con carne

Hams, Holland

Poultry/game products

Prepared meals:

Hungarian

Italian

Swedish

Tamales

MISC.

Dips/spreads, Mexican

Fruits in syrup, Greek

Greek specialties

Kosher products

Noodles, spinach

Pates

PICKLES, RELISHES

Capers

Kraut

Onions, pickled

Pickles:

dill

sweet

SOUPS, CHOWDERS

Bouillon/soup flavorings

Chowders/bisques

Soup mixes

Soups:

Chinese

cream

French

turtle

SPICES, SEASONINGS

Ginger

Paprika

Saffron

Salts

Seasonings/sauces

Vinegar

SYRUPS, TOPPINGS, BUTTERS

Apple butter

Honey, orange blossom

Jams/jellies/preserves, fruit

Jams/jellies/preserves, wine

Puddings/pudding mixes

Syrups, fruit

Syrups, maple

Toppings, dessert

VEGETABLES

Artichokes/artichoke hearts

Asparagus

Beans:

baked

green

red kidney

wax

Beets

CHARLOTTE CHARLES, INC. (Cont'd)

Carrots

Cauliflower/cauliflower products

Celery

Corn

Mushrooms

Onions

Peas

Peppers, jalapeno

Potatoes/potato products

Rice, white, wild

Sweet potatoes/yams

Tomatoes/tomato products

A gourmet's supermarket, Charlotte Charles offers nearly the most extensive selection of fine foods seen anywhere. Whether your tastes run toward stuffed peppers or to squid, you can be almost sure Charlotte Charles has it. They feature a list of vegetables that is unusually long for a mail order company and a unique line of prepared meals. The completeness of their offerings is Charlotte Charles' trademark, with herring fillets in six different sauces, twenty-four kinds of preserves, and fourteen varieties of olives, just to scratch the surface. They also have a good selection of gift packages featuring boxed combinations of their gourmet goodies.

32 page catalog free

CHEESE OF ALL NATIONS
153 Chambers St.
New York, N.Y. 10007

PRODUCTS:

Cheese:

Austria

Blue/bleu

Brie

Camembert

Cheddar

Colby

Coon

Cream

Edam

England

Finland

France

Germany

Goat's milk

Gouda

Gruyere

Hickory smoked

Holland

Ireland	Portugal
Israel	Provolone
Italy	Romanello
Limburger	Romano
Longhorn	Roumania
Low fat	Sheep's milk
Mexico	Spain
Monterey jack	Stilton
Mozzarella	Sweden
Muenster	Swiss
Norway	Switzerland
Parmesan	Tao foo
Pennsylvania Dutch	Tybo
Poland	Vermont
Port salut	Wisconsin
	Cheese products

Brilliat-Savarin, the noted French gastronomist, remarked, "A meal without cheese is like a day without sunshine." And at Phil Alpert's Cheese of All Nations it is sunny weather from Africa to Wales as they present over 1,000 varieties of cheeses from around the world. Where else could you order Czechoslovakian Olimintz, Icelandic Akyryrie and Vermont Cheddar all at once. The most knowledgeable gourmet would be hard-pressed to ask for a cheese that Phil Alpert's doesn't carry. They also have cheese spreads, gift packages, and a special selection of Kosher cheeses. The catalog from Cheese of All Nations is a trip in itself, with ideas, wine information, and such delightful trivia as, "Etiquette authorities tell us it is perfectly proper to eat the firmer cheeses with our fingers." So if you're into cheeses or want to be, then you can fly around the world with Cheese of All Nations and expect a rewarding experience.

CHICO-SAN, INC.
1144 W. 1st St.
Chico, Calif. 95926

PRODUCTS:

Beans, Japanese
Butter, sesame
Cakes, rice
Candy, rice
Cereals, rice
Chips, corn
Chips, rice
Flavoring essences
Flour, rice
Noodles:
   buckwheat
   whole wheat
Plums, prepared
Pumpkin seeds
Rice:
   brown
   sweet

Salts
Sesame oil
Soybeans
Starch, oriental cooking
Syrup, grain
Tamari soy sauce
Tea, herb
Vegetables, sea
Vinegar

An importer and manufacturer of oriental foods, Chico-San takes the macrobiotic approach in their selections. Chico-San's specialty, their rice cakes, are made from 100% whole grain brown rice and brown sesame seed, without chemicals or preservatives. They offer a long line of condiments featuring such things as soy sauce, soybean puree, sesame butter, salt plums and kozu. From the northern coast of Japan (not to be confused with the southern coast of Japan) comes a line of sea vegetables: hijiki, kombu, wakame. In addition to oriental foods, Chico-San also has cosmetics, books and utensils.

Catalog free

CHUCKWAGON FOODS
Micro Drive
Woburn, Mass. 01801

PRODUCTS:

Camping/storage foods

For the hunter, camper and other outdoorsman and out-
doorswoman, high nutrition, non-perishable, compact foods
are a necessity. At ChuckWagon, there is a good selection of
foods which meet the demands of those hardy souls who
venture into the wilds. One can either choose pre-packaged
meals or create his own combinations from a long list of
breakfast items, fruits, vegetables, soups, main dishes, snacks
and desserts. All combine light weight with high nutritional
value and have a guaranteed shelf life of twelve months.

Price list free

CLAMBAKE INTERNATIONAL, INC.
678 Massachusetts Ave., Suite 704
Cambridge, Mass. 02139

PRODUCTS:

Clams/clam products
Chowders/bisques
Lobsters/lobster products

Specializing in catered clambakes, Douglas Mann's Clambake
International will bring all the delights of this New England
tradition wherever you live. They will ship everything from

CLAMBAKE INTERNATIONAL, INC. (Cont'd)

the freshest seafood, chicken or steak to all the cooking facilities and trained cooks. For those who wish to do their own clambakes, they will send live lobsters, steamers and clam chowder anywhere in the world.

Descriptive brochure free

CROWLEY CHEESE, INC.
Healdville, Vt. 05147

PRODUCTS:

Cheese, Vermont

Crowley Cheese, Inc., is one of the few companies that still make cheese by hand. Vermont has long had an outstanding reputation for fine cheese, and at Crowley, which is the oldest cheese factory in Vermont, this tradition is carried on. The curds are still cut and raked by hand, using tools of the last century. They produce a Colby cheese, which is softer and smoother textured than a Cheddar, and age it to mild, medium or sharp taste.

Descriptive brochure and price list free

DAISYFRESH YOGURT CO.
P.O. Box 36
Santa Cruz, Calif. 95063

PRODUCTS:

Yogurt culture

You can't order a quart of yogurt from Daisyfresh, but you can certainly get everything you need to make your own. Starting with their Bulgarian yogurt culture, you can order containers, culturizers and recipe manuals for making from four quarts to three gallons at one time.

Price list free

DAKIN FARM
Rt. 7
Ferrisburg, Vt. 05456

PRODUCTS:

Cheese:
  cheddar
  hickory smoked
Honey, clover
Syrup, maple

From Dakin Farm in **Vermont** to customers all over the country have been sent over 18,000 cans of maple syrup and ten tons of Cheddar cheese. All their cheese is aged between 1 and 2½ years, whereas most cheese sold in stores today is only about 3 months old. Maple syrup fanciers can order from a pint to a gallon of pure Vermont flavor, canned at Dakin Farm. They also offer clover honey and three gift combinations.

Illustrated price list free

DEER VALLEY FARM
R.D. 1
Guilford, N.Y. 13780

PRODUCTS:

BAKERY GOODS

Bread:
  banana
  brown
  date nut
  raisin
  rye
  whole wheat
Buns:
  frankfurter/hamburger
  maple nut

Cakes:
  nut
  rice
  whole wheat
Cocktail snacks, corn
Cookies:
  butter
  molasses
  oatmeal
  peanut butter

DEER VALLEY FARM (Cont'd)

Crackers/wafers:
  cheese
  graham
  whole wheat
Danish pastries
Muffins
Pies:
  apple
  pineapple
  pumpkin
Toasts/crispbreads

CANDIES
Candy:
  honey
  horehound
  licorice
  nut
  slippery elm
Fudge

DAIRY PRODUCTS
Cheese:
  cheddar
  Swiss
  Wisconsin
Milk, powdered
Whey/whey products
Yogurt
Yogurt culture

HERBS, SEASONINGS, SPICES
Agar-agar
Basil
Cayenne
Chervil
Cinnamon
Coriander

Curry
Garlic
Herbs, aromatic
Horseradish
Marjoram
Mustard
Nutmeg
Oregano
Parsley
Rosemary
Sage
Salts
Tarragon
Thyme

FLOURS, MEALS, CEREALS
Baking powders/yeasts
Cereals:
  barley
  mixed
  ready to serve
Groats
Meals, baking/cooking
Flour:
  barley
  graham
  oat
  potato
  rice
  rye
  wheat
  white
Oatmeal
Pancake mixes
Wheat germ/wheat germ products

DEER VALLEY FARM (Cont'd)

FRUITS, NUTS
- Applesauce
- Apples, fresh
- Banana products
- Carob/carob products
- Cherries, red
- Coconuts/coconut products
- Cranberry sauce
- Fruit, dried
- Grapefruit, fresh
- Nuts
- Oranges, fresh
- Papaya products
- Peaches, prepared
- Peanuts:
  - raw
  - roasted
- Pecans/pecan products
- Pineapple products
- Pumpkins
- Raspberries

JELLIES, SYRUPS, SWEETENERS
- Flavoring essences
- Honey:
  - imported
  - tupelo
  - wild flower
- Jams/jellies/preserves:
  - berry
  - fruit
  - herb
- Molasses
- Sugar:
  - brown
  - date

Syrups:
- fruit
- grain
- maple

JUICES, BEVERAGES
Juice:
- berry
- fruit
- vegetable

Tea, herb

MISC.
- Food supplements/vitamins
- Ketchup/catsup
- Kraut
- Mustards
- Noodles:
  - macaroni
  - spaghetti
- Tamari soy sauce
- Vinegar

OILS, BUTTERS, SPREADS
- Butters/spreads, nut
- Margarine
- Oils, vegetable
- Peanut butter
- Salad dressings

SOUPS, RELISHES, SAUCES
- Beef stew
- Bouillon/soup flavorings
- Chili con carne
- Chow chow
- Hash, beef
- Pickles, dill
- Relishes

Soups:
  beef
  vegetable
Spaghetti sauce

VEGETABLES, SEEDS
Beans:
  green
  lima
  pinto
  red kidney
Beets
Carrots
Corn
Lentils

Peas
Peas, split
Popcorn
Pumpkin seeds
Rice:
  brown
  Italian
  wild
Sesame seeds
Soybeans
Soybean products
Sunflower seeds
Tomatoes/tomato products
Vegetables, sea

Devoted to organic farming since 1947, Deer Valley Farm offers top quality natural foods. With everything from baked goods to fruit to spices, their list seems very extensive. All products are guaranteed to be free of chemicals and prservatives.

DE SOUSA'S – THE HEALTHIANS
2376 Orangethorpe Ave.
Anaheim, Calif. 92806

PRODUCTS:

Apple butter
Food supplements/vitamins
Ginseng/ginseng products

Jams/jellies/preserves, fruit
Juice, fruit
Salad dressings

Tea, mint

This health-oriented company stocks a line of products that are completely free from harmful chemicals and additives. In addition to their juices and preserves, they also offer vitamin

28

E in cream, oil, capsule and tablet forms, a shampoo and skin cleaner, as well as such items as mink lotion, golden seal and salt of the earth.

Price list free

DIAMOND DAIRY GOAT FARM
Route 2
Portage, Wisc. 53901

PRODUCTS:

Cheese, goat's milk   Milk, goat

Goat milk and cheese are Diamond Dairy's sole products. The cheese is sold either salt-free or lightly salted and is made entirely from goat milk. The goats are fed entirely on organic feedstuffs on the Diamond Dairy Goat Farm.

Brochure free

EMBASSY SEAFOODS
P.O. Box 165
Gloucester, Mass. 01930

PRODUCTS:

Cheese, Vermont
Clams/clam products
Crabs/crab products   Salmon/salmon products
Finnan haddie   Sardines/sardine products
Fish chowder   Roe
Lobster bisque   Shrimp/shrimp products
Lobsters/lobster products   Syrup, maple
Newburg sauce   Tuna/tuna products

EMBASSY SEAFOODS (Cont'd)

Embassy captures the ocean-fresh taste of seafood with fish and lobster from colorful Gloucester and North Atlantic fishing boats which moor just a few steps away, allowing Embassy to start with just-caught goodness. Their dips and spreads are made from selected lobsters, shrimps, clams and smoked fish, combined with cream cheese, sherry or Worcestershire sauce, ready to serve as dips with chips and crackers, or use to stuff celery. In addition to their dips, spreads and chowders, they offer salt mackerel and cud cured in the traditional way handed down among seafarers for 300 years. The New England taste of their seafood is also accented in their Vermont cheese and maple syrup.

Illustrated brochure and price list free. They also offer a special list of gift assortments

EMPIRE COFFEE AND TEA COMPANY
486 9th Ave.
New York, N.Y. 10018

PRODUCTS:

Allspice	Jamaican
Anise	Java
Chamomile	Kenya
Chicory	Mexico
Cloves	mocha
Coffee:	Tanzania
blends	Turkey
Brazil	unroasted
Colombia	Venezuela
Costa Rica	Fennel
decaffienated	Garlic powder
French roast	Herbs, blended
Hawaiian	Linden
instant	Malva
Italian roast	Onion powder

English	Pepper, black
Formosa	Pepper, white
green	Peppermint
Irish	Tea:
jasmine	black
lapsang souchong	blends
mint	Ceylon
oolong	Chinese People's Republic
orange pekoe	darjeeling
verbena	Earl Gray

Empire Coffee and Tea Company, long a favorite stopover for New Yorkers, offers forty types of coffee and thirty-eight different kinds of tea. Their coffees can be obtained in any grind or in bean form. They will also blend to order. Their teas can be ordered loose or in bags, and can also be blended to order.

ESTEE CANDY CO., INC.
169 Lackawanna Ave.
Parrsippany, N.J. 07054

PRODUCTS:

Dietetic products

Estee Candy Company, Inc., **manufactures a line of dietetic** sweets and biscuits that includes gum drops, hard candies, chocolate bars, gum, cookies and wafers. They are manufactured primarily for those on sugar and salt restricted diets. Made without sugar or artificial sweeteners, Estee products present an alternative to sugar sweets and compare favorably in taste and appearance.

Catalog free

THE FMALI CO.
P.O. Box 1072
Santa Cruz, Calif. 95061

PRODUCTS:

Ginseng/ginseng products
Goldenseal

This company specializes in oriental herbs, medicinals and sundries. They sell to distributors and retailers, and have a wholesale mail-order clientele as well. Most of their products are imported from mainland China, although some roots and teas are American.

Catalog free

THE FORSTS
CPO Box P
Kingston, N.Y. 12401

PRODUCTS:

Apples, McIntosh
Bacon, smoked
Braunschweiger   Salami
Canadian bacon   Sausage, smoked
Ham, smoked   Steak, filet mignon
Pheasant, smoked   Steak, strip
                        Turkey, smoked

The Forsts have been operating since 1861, so they should know good meats. And a mouth-watering selection it is, with smoked pheasant, turkey, bacon and other fine meats from the Catskill Mountains. They also have gift assortments, gift certificates and club memberships.

Price list free

GRACE TEA CO., LTD.
799 Broadway
New York, N.Y. 10003

PRODUCTS:

Tea:
  blends
  Ceylon
  darjeeling
  Earl Gray
  English
  Formosa
  jasmine
  lapsang souchong
  oolong

Purveyors to tea connoisseurs, Grace Tea Company combines superb and rare teas from around the world to offer their own unique blends as well as the best singles. From England, Ceylon or Formosa, the teas offered are bound to be the best, selected by experts.

Catalog free

GREAT VALLEY MILLS, INC.
101 S. West End Blvd. (Rt. 309)
Quakertown, Pa. 18951

PRODUCTS:

Bacon
Beef, dried
Bologna:
  beer
  Lebanon
  ring
Canadian bacon

Cheese:
  bleu
  cheddar
  Edam
  Gouda
  Pennsylvania Dutch
Chili sauce
Chow-chow
Corn meal
Corn relish
Flour:
  buckwheat
  rye
  soy bean
  white
  whole wheat
Ham, smoked
Honey:
  Haycock Mountain
  honeysuckle
Hot cake/waffle mix
Maple butter
Molasses:
  blackstrap
  colonial

Oat groats
Oatmeal:
  Irish
  Scotch
Peach butter
Pickles, bread and butter
Preserves:
  apricot
  blackberry
  blueberry
  cherry
  fig
  orange marmalade
  peach
  pear
  pineapple
  raspberry
  strawberry
  tomato
Quince butter
Sausage, smoked
Scrapple
Tongue, smoked
Turkey, smoked
Wheat germ

A mail order company with customers in all 50 states, Great Valley Mills features stone ground flours, whole grain flours, pancake mixes, cereals, smoked hams and bacons, and Pennsylvania Dutch preserves and butters. These are all products of the Pennsylvania Dutch countryside, shipped world wide and year round.

Catalog free

THE HERB LADY
P.O. Box 26515
Los Angeles, Calif. 90026

PRODUCTS:

Cayenne
Chamomile
Comfrey
Damiana
Fennel seeds
Fenugreek
Fu-tze powder
Ginseng/ginseng products
Goldenseal
Gotu Cola
Kola nut powder
Passion flower

Peppermint
Sarsaparilla root
Sassafras bark
Skullcap
Tea, blends
Valerian root
Yohimbe bark

The Herb Lady has a fair offering of herbs, ginseng and tea blends. While not as extensive as some, her list contains the most popular types, such as chamomile, gotu-kola, peppermint and sassafras. Going by the motto, "Herbs for the Highest Good," the Herb Lady conveys genuine concern for people's health.

Price list free

JAFFE BROS. NATURAL FOODS
P.O. Box 636
Valley Center, Calif. 92082

PRODUCTS:

Almond butter
Almonds
Avacados
Carob/carob produc
Cashews

Dates	Oranges
Filbert nuts	Peanuts, Spanish
Fruit, dried	Pecans
Juice, berry	Soybeans
Juice, fruit	Soy flour
Lemons	Walnuts
Macadamia nuts	Whole wheat berries

This is a twenty-five year old family business, operating from their own ranch. Everything is grown organically and un-fumigated. Of special interest are their selection of dates and their seed and nut butters.

Price list free

V. W. JOYNER & COMPANY
315 Main St.
Smithfield, Va. 23430

PRODUCTS:

Hams, Smithfield

Smithfield hams are not like other hams. They have a distinctive flavor, texture and color which sets them apart. V. W. Joyner & Company still use the old smoking methods used when the company was founded in the 19th century. The process produces a unique and delicious ham.

Color brochure (with recipes and instructions for proper cooking) free

KAKAWATEEZ, LIMITED
130 Olive St.
Findlay, Ohio 45840

PRODUCTS:

Almonds
Brazil nuts
Cashews
Filbert nuts
Macadamia nuts
Peanuts, roasted
Pistachios

They produce and distribute dry-roasted nuts covered with a unique coating. Distribution covers most areas of the United States and several foreign countries. Their special coating process was discovered in old Mexico and contains no fats or oils.

Catalog free

K. KALUSTYAN
123 Lexington Ave.
New York, N.Y. 10016

PRODUCTS:

Agarbatti
Bombay duck
Chillies
Chutney
Coconut
Dalls

Flour:
  graham
  rice
  wheat
Mint
Pickles
Rice
Varian

An unusual selection of foodstuffs—Armenian, Indian, Pakistani, Turkish, Iranian. Whether one's taste runs to Basmatti rice, Agarbatti or garlic chutney, this is the place.

Catalog 25¢ with pre-addressed envelope

KAM SHING CO.
2246 S. Wentworth
Chicago, Ill. 60616

芝城 司公盛金 美國

KAM SHING COMPANY

PRODUCTS:

Abalone, Mexican

Agar agar

Bamboo shoots

Cuttlefish, seasoned

Duck egg, salted

Egg noodles

Egg rolls

Fish stomach, fried

Five spice powder

Fungus, dried

Lychee nuts

Mustard greens, preserved

Mustard greens, salted

Quong Hap Ben cake

Radish, preserved

Rice sticks

Rice, sweet

Sea cucumber

Seaweed, dried

Sesame oil

Sesame paste

Shark's fin

Shrimp chips

Soybean curd

Soy sauce, H.K.

Soy Sauce, Kikoman

Subgum, sweet

Vinegar, black

Water chestnuts

Many exotic foods from Hong Kong, Taiwan, the Philippines and Thailand. There are very few companies which supply many of these oriental foods. They also have cooking utensils, such as Chinese cooking pans, choppers and a rice cooker.

Price list free

KATAGIRI & CO., INC.
224 E. 59th St.
New York, N.Y. 10022

PRODUCTS:

Ajitsukenori

Akadashi

Amanatto

Amazu-Shoga

Aonoriko

Ao Uzumaki Fu

Arare:

Goma

Hana

Kaki no Tane

Norimaki

38

Asakusanori
Azuki
Benishoga
Bonchiage
Bull dog sauce
Bull dog Tonkatsu sauce
California Blue Rose
Calpis
Chidori Senbei
Chirimenzako (Iriko)
Chukasoba
Curry powder
Daikaku Okaki
Daizu
Dashizako (Iriko)
Dashikobu
Dashi-No-Moto
Eiyoni
Flave
Fujiya Milky
Funyu (US)
Furikakenori
Furikane Nori
Fujimoto, white (US)
Genmaicha
Goma Shio
Goma (Shvio, Kuro)
Gyokuro
Habucha
Hachimitsu
Hajikami
Hanakatsuo
Hanarakkyo
Harihari-Zuke
Harusame/Sai Fun (China)
Harvest Gomairi Biscuit

Hawaii Sanbaizuke (US)
Hawaii Takuwan
Hayanikobu
Hijiki
Hi-Me
Hiyamugi
Hoshiebi
Hoshi Renkon (China)
Ichimi Togarashi
Ika Shiokara
Ikari sauce
Ikarimame
Indian curry, house
Iro Ichiban
Isago Senbei
Itokezuri Hanakatsuo
Itowakame
Japan Takuwan
Jintan
Joshinko
Junsai
Kagome sauce
Kagome Tonkatsu sauce
Kakimochi
Kakukiri Kobu
Kampyo
Kanten (Shiro or Aka)
Kappa Tengoku (Kyuri)
Karashi Kobu
Katakuriko
Katsuo Mirinyaki
Katsuodenbu
Katsuo Dashi-No-Moto
Katsuo Shiokara
Kaurayanagi Bancha
Kewpie Mayonnaise

Kinako

Kishimen (Shimodaya)

Kisoba (Ninben)

Kizami Surume

Kizamikobu

Koaji

Kobu-Ame

Kobucha

Kobumaki

Kodai

Kokuho

Kompeito

Koshian

Koumezuke

Koyadofu

Kunsei

Kuromame

Kyuri-No-Kyuchan

Maruboshi Iuwashi

Menma

Midori-No-Kaori (Sencha)

Mirinboshi Iwashi

Mizuyokan

Mochigome (US)

Mochiko (US)

Monaka-No-Kawa

Mugicha

Mustard (S&B)

Nagasaki Chanpon

Namawakame

Nametake Ajitsuke

Narazuke

Narazuke (Chuyu)

Narazuke (Kyuri)

Narazuke (Uri)

Nihon Su (Mitsukan)

Nikke Senbei

Nishimekobu

Nori/Ajitsuke (Yamagataya)

Nori Fumi

Nori Senbei

Nori Tamago

Nori Tsukudani

Nuka

Nukamiso-No-Moto

Oborokobu

Ochazukenori

Okaka

Okonomiyaki

Okonomizuke Shoga

Okoshi

Oshimugi

Panko

Pepper, house

Ponzu

Powdered tea

Rakkyo

Ryokoume (Satozuke)

Saki-Ika Ajitsuke

Sakura Ienbu

Sakuraebi

Salad Usuyaki Arare

Salmon Kasuzuke

Salmon, salted

Sansho powder

Sasakarei Hoshi

Sashimi Shoyu

S&B Table Kosho

Senbonzuke

Sencha

Sendai

Sengiri Daikon

Sesame oil (Goma)

Shichimi Togarashi

Shinshu

Shio-Endo

Shiitake (Ashikiri)

Shiitake-Iri-Kobu

Shinano Soba

Shiokobu

Shiratamako

Shisonajimi

Shisononi-Zuke

Shoga-No-Ko, powdered

Shoga Senbei

Somen

Sukimidara

Sukiyaki Furikake

Sukonbu

Surume

Sushisu (Mitsukan)

Suzuki

Suzuko Kasuzuke

Tarako Shiozuke

Tea bags

Tempurako

Tempura mix

Tempura sauce (base)

Teriyaki sauce

Tororokobu

Tsujiura (Fortune) Senbei

Tsukudani

Tsuyu-No-Moto (Ninben)

Udon-Kaku (Shimodaya)

Umeboshi

Umeboshi Chazuke

Ume Amazuke

Ume Kobucha

Unineri

Vermont curry, house

Wakame

Wasabiko

Yachiyo Fa

Yaki-Ika Ajitsuke

Yakinori Sushimaki

Yamagataya Sencha

Yamajirushi

Yamasa Shimmi

Yamasa Shoyu

Yamatoyaki (Shio Senbei)

Yokan (Kuri, Neri, Azuki, cha,
    Kintsuba, Kaki)

Yosaburozuke (Nasu)

Yoshinokuzu

Zenmai

Retail and mail order on exotic Japanese foods. Katagiri has quite a unique list of items, ranging from Bull Dog sauce to Umeboshi. The knowledgeable connoisseur of oriental edibles will be quite pleased at the many hard-to-find favorites. They also carry cooking utensils and popular Japanese magazines.

Price list free

KOINONIA PRODUCTS
Rt. 1
Americus, Ga. 31709

PRODUCTS:

Carob/carob products
Fruitcake
Pecans

Koinonia Farm was established in 1942 as a cooperative effort in scientific farming, making significant contributions to the surrounding area. After surviving years of hostility brought on by their stand against racial prejudice, they are today a highly organized group using their money and energy for much social good. Koinonia offers pecans, available in the shell, shelled, spiced, hickory smoked, or in dates. They also have carob pecan candy and fruitcake.

Catalog free

L. & L. HEALTH FOODS CO.
Rt. 1 Box 197
Fairview, Okla. 73737

PRODUCTS:

Carob/carob products	Popcorn
Dates	Prunes
Figs	Pumpkin seeds
Flour:	Raisins
oat	Rice, brown
rice	Sesame seeds
rye	Soya flour
wheat	Soybeans
Peanut butter	Sunflower seeds
Peanuts, raw	Walnuts
Pecans	Wheat germ/wheat germ products

Organically grown wheat and stone-ground flour of their own production. They carry those foods normally stocked by health food outlets. They also offer vitamin capsules and tablets.

Price list free

LA NORMA COFFEE MILLS, INC.
4416 N. Hubert Ave.
Tampa, Fla. 33614

PRODUCTS:

no list given

Mail order gourmet coffees—any blend, any roast, any grind or in the bean. Packaged in cellophane packages or vacuum tins. Also mail order antique-style coffee grinders and a variety of coffee makers.

Information free on request

LEE'S FRUIT CO., INC.
Box 450
Leesburg, Fla. 32748

PRODUCTS:

Grapefruit	satsuma
Honey, orange blossom	temple
Oranges:	Tangelos
navel	Watermelon

Citrus fruits and watermelon grown with composting methods which yield high nutritional values. Availability of each type of fruit is, of course, seasonal. Unfortunately, state laws prevent shipment of Florida citrus into California, Arizona and Texas unless the fruit has been fumigated, which Lee's is not.

Price list free

LES ECHALOTTES
Ramsey, N.J. 07446

PRODUCTS:

Abalone
Abalone in soy sauce
All beef cocktail frankfurters
All beef cocktail meatballs
All beef cocktail salami
All beef salami
Almond macaroon
Anchovies, rolled
Anchovy paste
Antipasto
Apricot preserves
Artichoke bottoms
Artichoke hearts
Assorted fruits in Jamaican rum
Bamboo pickle
Bamboo shoots
Bean soup with potatoes
Bearnaise sauce
Bengal Club, Indian chutney
Bird's nest soup
Bitter orange marmalade
Biscuit assortment

Bisque:
    crab
    crawfish
    lobster
    shrimp
Blackberry jelly
Black currant jelly
Black cherry preserves
Boiled baby clams
Bombay ducks
Bouillabaisse soup
Bouquet garni
Brandied cherries
Brandy cakes
Brandy flavor
Brandy sauce
Bulgar
Bumbu Nasi Goreng (mixed
    spices & onions)

Calf's foot jelly

Capers

Carrots

Cassis (black currant)

Celery knobs, sliced

Cepes

Ceylon breakfast tea

Champagne biscuits

Chanterelles

Cheese souffle

Chestnut stuffing

Chestnuts, whole, in brine

Chick peas

Chili bean dip

Chili con queso

Chocolate souffle

Cocktail frankfurters, Danish

Coconut syrup

Colman mustard, French

Colman mustard, hot English

Colonel Skinner, Indian chutney

Coquillettes

Couscous

Cream of vichyssoise soup

Creme de marrons

Crepe Suzette

Crystallized assorted flowers

Crystallized ginger, sliced

Crystallized lilacs

Crystallized mint leaves

Crystallized rose petals

Crystallized violets

Crystallized whole red rose

Currant sponge pudding

Curried beef pie with gravy

Curry paste

Curry powder

Curry sauce

Curry, standard instant

Darjeeling tea

Date sponge pudding

Dijon pudding

Dutch gaufrettes

Earl Grey tea

Enchilada sauce

Enchiladas, cheese

Endives

English breakfast tea

English mustard

English sponge pudding

Escargots

Escoffier sauce

Espresso coffee, Motta

Falernum

Filet of anchovies

Filet of tuna

Fire cherries in brandy

Fish chowder

Foie gras, natural

Formosa oolong tea

French asparagus

French choucroute

French liver pate

French mustard

French onion soup

French wafers

Fried chili paste

Fried Java noodle dish
  (Bahmi Goreng)

Fried onions

Fruitcake, old Irish whiskey

Gherkins in vinegar

Ginger preserves

Ginger, preserved stem

Ginger sponge pudding

Golden syrup sponge pudding

Graisse d'Oie

Grapefruit marmalade

Green chili, peeled

Green flageolets

Grenadine

Ground beef with onion pie

Hard sauce

Harissa, hot pepper spread

Hearts of palm

Homard sauce

Hot mango, Indian chutney

Hot mango kasoondie

Hot mango pickle

Hot orange peel pickle

Irish breakfast tea

Irish mushroom sauce

Irish salad dressing

Israeli gefilte fish

Jasmine tea

Java chili paste

Java fried rice dish

Java soy sauce (Ketjap Benteng)

Jellied eel

Keemun China tea

King crabmeat

Kippered herring

Lapsang souchong tea

Leeks

Lemon marmalade

Lentil soup with potatoes

Lime marmalade

Lime pickle

Linzer torte with ground almonds

Lobster paste

Lobster souffle

Lychee nuts

Macadamia nuts

Mackerels marinated with wine

Madiera sauce

Major Grey Indian chutney

Marmalade, coarse cut

Marmalade sponge pudding

Marron glaces

Marrons, broken, in syrup

Marrons in vanilla syrup

Marzipan

Medaglia d'Oro espresso coffee

Mexican style beans

Mincemeat with brandy

Mint cakes

Mint jelly

Mint syrup

Mixed fruit sponge pudding

Mixed vegetable soup

Mock turtle soup

Morilles

Mushrooms, freeze-dried

Mushroom soup

Mussels

Mussels fried in butter

Mussels on the half shell

Nantua sauce

Old English mince pie

Olive oil, French

Orange flower water

Orange pekoe black tea

Orgeat, almond syrup

Oxtail soup

Painsol

Palm leaves

Pappadums wafers

Pate a go go

Pate de campagne

Pate de foie du perigord

Pate du chef Francais

Pate du perigord

Pate Maison Truffe

Pate, truffled

Peanut oil, pure

Pea soup with potatoes

Peppers, red & yellow

Perigueux sauce

Petit babs in rum

Petite beurre

Pickled eel

Pickled walnut

Pike dumplings Nantua

Pike dumplings naturel,
    Quenelles

Pinto beans

Plum pudding

Polenta, instant

Prince of Wales tea

(Puree) de Foie Gras with
    Truffles

Puree de marrons naturel

Quail eggs

Queen Mary's tea

Quenelles of veal with
    mushroom sauce

Quenelles of veal naturel

Quince jelly

Rairgote sauce

Raspberry & red currant jelly

Raspberry preserves

Raynal & Roquelaure

Red currant jelly

Red currant preserves

Red salmon caviar

Re-frying beans

Romanoff cocktail pate

Rose petal jelly

Rose water

Rose wine vinegar

(Roulade) of foie gras with
    truffles

Roulade of ham

Rum cakes

Rum sauce

Salmon, sliced/smoked

Salsify

Sardines

Sauce cumberland

Sauce diable

Sauce melba

Sauce Robert

Sauerkraut, wine flavored

Scotch whiskey marmalade

Sea salt

Seasoning for snails

Shad roe

Shark's fin soup

Shrimp wafers

Smoked baby clams

Smoked eel

Smoked eel fillets

Smoked oysters

Smoked sturgeon

Snail soup

Snow peas

Sorrel

Soup bags/flavorings

Sour cherry preserves

Spratts in oil

Steak & chop sauce

Steak & kidney pie

Steak & mushroom pie

Strasbourg pate maison

Strasbourg smoked goose pate
   d'Oie Fumee

Strawberry preserves

Stringless beans

Stuffed vine leaves

Sturgeon caviar

Sultana sponge pudding

Swiss fondeu

Swiss fondeu, rarebit

Taco sauce

Tapioca

Tarragon leaves in vinegar
   estragon

Tarragon vinegar

Terrine Bordelaise au vin de
   sauternes

Terrines do foie gras with
   truffles

Tomato soup

Tortillas, canned

Tricoulor Orleans mustard

Tripes

Truffles

Turkey, mixed dark & white

Turtle soup

Urbani truffles

Vanilla souffle

Venison casserle

Walnut oil

Water chestnuts

Watercress soup

Wheat pilaf

White flageolets

Whole beef tongue, cooked

A fine selection of gourmet foods imported from France.
They also have such delicacies as sturgeon caviar from Iran
and anchovies from Portugal. Their main emphasis, however,
is on the shallots, which are milder than garlic and quite
popular in France. Of course the gourmet will have no trouble
finding truffles, tripes, soups and sauces at Les Echalottes

Catalog 25¢

48

LHASA KARNAK HERB CO.
2482 Telegraph Ave.
Berkeley, Calif. 94704

PRODUCTS:

Agrimony
Alfalfa
Allspice
Angelica
Anise
Arrowroot
Balm of Gilead
Basil
Bayberry bark
Bay leaves
Birch bark
Bloodroot
Caraway
Cardamon
Cayenne
Centaury herb
Chamomile
Chaparral
Chervil
Chicory
Cinnamon
Cloves
Cola nuts
Coltsfoot
Comfrey
Coriander
Damiana
Dill
Elder bark
Eyebright
Fennel seed
Fenugreek seed
Garlic

Ginger
Ginseng
Goldenrod
Goldenseal
Gota Kola
Gum Arabic
Horehound
Irish Moss
Juniper berries
Lady's Mantle
Lavender flowers
Licorice root
Linden
Lobelia
Mace
Marjoram
Mugwort
Nutmeg
Oregano
Paprika
Parsley
Passion Flower
Pepper, black
Pepper, white
Peppermint
Periwinkle
Poppy seeds
Raspberry leaves
Rose hips
Rosemary
Saffron
Sage
Sarsaparilla root

Sassafras bark	Uva Ursi leaves
Skullcap	Valarian root
Spearmint	Vervain
Tea, blends	Walnut leaves
Thyme	Yarrow
Turmeric	

A retail and mail order herb and spice company. In addition to carrying a comprehensive line of herbs for cooking and healing, they specialize in blended herb teas, herbal smoking mixtures, bath herbs, and a wide selection of ginseng and ginseng products. They welcome inquiries about wholesale discounts on bulk purchases.

Catalog free

LONE ORGANIC FARM
Rt. 1 Box 58
Millersburg, Ind. 46543

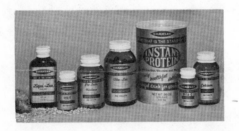

PRODUCTS:

Comfrey
Food supplements

The Lone Organic Farm is run by Mr. Moses J. Troyer, a man who seems genuinely concerned about healthful living. Live comfrey roots are available by mail and all products are free from chemicals and additives. This is a small business and they have no catalog.

MAGIC GARDEN HERB CO.
P.O. Box 332
Fairfax, Calif. 94930

PRODUCTS:

Mormon Tea

Alfalfa leaves
Allspice
Aloe gum
Angelica root
Asafoetida gum
Areca & Catechu
Apricot kernels
Balmony herb
Basil leaves
Bayberry bark
Bay leaves
Bardana root
Benzoin gum
Beth root
Bistort root
Black Cohosh root
Blackhaw   Blackhaw
Blessed Thistle
Bittersweet
Blue Cohosh root
Borage
Bugleweed
Cascara bark
Caraway
Capiscum
Cardamon seeds
Celandine
Chamomile
Chickweed
Chiretta
Cinchona bark
Cloves
Columbo root

Coriander seeds
Comfrey
Cramp bark
Cubeb berries
Cumin seeds
Damiana leaves
Dill seeds
Dulse
Elder flowers
Eucalyptus leaves
Fennel seeds
Fenugreek seeds
Frankincense
Germander
Ginger root
Ginseng (Korean)
Ginseng (Chinese)
Gotu Kola
Goldenseal root
Guaiac wood
Henna leaves
Herbal facial
Herbal tobacco

Hops

Horsetail

Hydrocotyle (Fo-ti-tieng)

Juniper berries

Kava Kava root

Kelp

Kola nut

Kino root

Lemon Verbena

Licorice root

Life Root

Lobelia

Lovage root

Marigold petals

Marjoram

Mate leaves

Matico leaves

Mistletoe

Mormon Tea

Motherwort

Mullein leaves

Muirapuama bark

Musk root

Myrrh

Nettle leaves

Nutmeg

Oregano

Papaya leaves

Passion Flower

Patchouly leaves

Peppermint

Pine resin

Pocan Bush

Potpourri

Quassia chips

Raspberry leaves

Rose hips

Rosemary

Sage

Sandalwood

Sarsaparilla root

Saw Palmetto berries

Scotch Broom

Sea Wrack

Skullcap

Smart Weed

Speedwell

Spikenard root

Squaw Weed

Stoneroot

Strawberry leaves

Tarragon

Thyme

Valerian root

White Oak bark

Witch Grass

Wormwood

Wood Betony

Yohimbe bark

Yuma Root

A company that offers not only a long list of herbs and information on their lore and uses, but also creams and oils for bathing and skin care, books, and nicotine-free smoking mixtures.

MANGANARO FOODS
488 9th Ave.
New York, N.Y. 10018

PRODUCTS:

All brands pasta
Almond paste
Amaretti
Amaro mineral water
Anchovies
Anchovies, salt
Anchovy paste
Anguila
Anisette coffee
Artichoke hearts
Asiago cheese

Asparagus
Avorio
Baba-Ferrara
Baby clams
Baby Gouda cheese
Baccala
Baci
Beans, stringless
Bel Paese cheese
Beluga
Biscuits for cheese
Bitterino mineral water
Black caviar
Bleu cheese
Bon Bel cheese
Bouillabaisse soup
Bread sticks
Brioschi
Cacciocavallo cheese
Calamares
Calamata olives
Camembert cheese

Caponatina
Cappelletti
Caramels
Carrots, miniature
Casalinga style
Cascado red
Caviar
Cheddar, Canada
Cheddar cheese
Cherries in brandy
Chestnut flour
Chick-pea flour
Chinotto mineral water
Citterio salami
Clos du Verdet
Cocktail biscuits
Colomba
Confetti
Coppa
Cotechini
Creme cassis

Curry, risotto

Domestic lion cheese

Dried chestnuts

Dry mushrooms

Edam cheese

Egg noodles

Emmentaler cheese

Endives

Escargots

Fernet Branca

Ferrara

Ferro China Bisleir

Figs

Fillet of tuna

Fiore Sardo cheese

Flageolets

Fonduta cheese

Fontina cheese

French Fontina cheese

French Gruyere cheese

French honey

French mustard

French syrup

French tuna

French vinegar

Frend Grielles

Fruilana cheese

Fruit in brandy

Gaeta olives

Gherkins

Gianduiotti

Ginger mineral water

Gorgonzola cheese

Green noodles

Home-made noodles

Incannestrata cheese

Instant demitasse

Instant gnocchi

Italian honey

Italian vinegar

Jacob's water biscuits

Jam or roses

Lemon mineral water

Lentils, baked

Lubisc

Lumpfish caviar

Mackerel

Maimone

Manganaros demitasse

Mantecha cheese

Marinated mussels

Marrons in syrup

Medaglia d'Oro

Milanese risotto

Milanese style antipasto

Minestrone

Mixed vegetables

Mortadella cheese

Mostarda

Motta espresso

Motta & Perugina

Motta syrup

Mozzarella cheese

Mushrooms

Mushrooms, Cepes, natural

Mushrooms, risotto

Mussels

Olives, plain, ripe, Italian

Olives, Spanish Queen, dry cured

Orange mineral water

Pancetta

Pandoro

Panettone
Panforte
Papaya
Parmesano cheese
Parodi sardines
Pasta Barilla
Pasta con Sarde
Pasta Fagiola
Pastene
Pate
Peas
Pecorino di Tavola cheese
Pecorino Romano cheese
Pepato cheese
Pepperoni
Pesto alla Genovese
Pignoli
Pimentos
Pitted wild cherries
Polenta, instant, Italian
Port Salut cheese
Proscuitto
Proscuittino
Provolerti cheese
Provolone cheese
Ragusano cheese
Ratatouille
Red clam sauce
Red & yellow peppers
Rice, Arborio
Ricotta cheese
Ricotta Romano cheese
Ricotta Siciliano cheese

Roasted peppers
Roquefort cheese
Saffron
Salami
Salami alla Cacciatora
Salsify
Sardines
Sauterne, domestic, vinegar
Scungilli
Smoked oysters
Snail gift set
Sopressata
Spinach lasagne
Spinach noodles
Stuffed cherry peppers
Stuffed manicotti
Swiss Fontina cheese
Swiss Gruyere cheese
Swiss Knight cheese
Taleggio cheese
Tea, chamomile
Terrines foie gras
Tomatoes
Tomatoes, risotto
Torrone
Tripes
Truffles, black
Tuna fish
Ventrasca
Vegetable jardiniere
Vivo coffee
Zampino

A New York landmark with a distinctive "old world" atmosphere, Manganero's is filled with mostly Italian ham, cheeses,

MANGANARO FOODS (Cont'd)

meats, and thousands of other fine gourmet foods. They specialize in hard-to-obtain items, their buyers visiting Italy several times a year to seek out new products. They also carry a line of utensils and gadgets for those who delight in old-world cookery.

Catalog free

McARTHUR'S SMOKEHOUSE, INC.
Millerton, N.Y. 12546

PRODUCTS:

Bacon, smoked
Canadian bacon
Capon, smoked
Corned beef
Game hen, smoked
Ham, smoked
Lamb, smoked

Sausage, smoked
Trout, smoked

McArthur's Smokehouse was established in 1876 and has maintained high quality in their products. They have remained small in order to prevent any semblance of assembly line operation. Their Canadian roast, smoked capon and smoked trout would be hard to find elsewhere. The discriminating gourmet can have a unique experience through McArthur's.

Catalog free

NEWFOUNDLAND BOOK & BIBLE HOUSE
106 Freshwater Rd.
St. Johns, Newfoundland, Canada

PRODUCTS:

Vegetarian meat substitutes

They are a small concern and may not carry everything, but have a good supply of those items for which they have had demand. Mostly, they are concerned with getting protein value from vegetables rather than meat, and offer meat substitutes to those who prefer vegetarian dining.

No catalog, but will answer any inquiries

NORTHWESTERN COFFEE MILLS
217 N. Broadway
Milwaukee, Wisc. 53202

PRODUCTS:

Coffee:	
blends	instant
Brazil	Java
Colombia	mocha
decaffienated	Tea:
French roast	black
	blends

Ceylon	green
Darjeerling	jasmine
Earl Grey	Lapsang souchong
English	oolong
Formosa	

These people know a lot about coffee and tea and they import the finest the world has to offer. Some of their coffees are readily available, some are scarce, and some are rare. Both their coffees and their teas are available either as "straights" or blended to achieve different taste sensations. They also have a fine list of herbs, spices and seasonings.

Catalog free

OLD TOWN NATURAL FOODS
174 Bridge St.
Las Vegas, N.M. 87701

PRODUCTS:

Agar agar	Chamomile
Alfalfa leaves	Chaparral
Angelica root	Chickweed
Anise seed	Chicory root, roasted
Apricots	Cilantro seed
Bayberry bark, powdered	Comfrey leaves
Beans, lima	Coltsfoot
Beans, pinto	Currants
Beans, red kidney	Damiana
Black Cohosh root	Dandelion root
Blue Cohosh root	Elder blossoms
Blue Vervain	Eucalyptus leaves
Burdock root	Fenugreek seeds
Calamus root	
Carob/carob products	
Catnip	

Flour:

   rye

   soy

   wheat

Fruit, dried

Goldenseal root, powdered

Gotu Kola

Green tea

Hibiscus flowers

Hops

Hyssop

Kota

Kinikinick (Uva Ursi)

Lavender

Lemon Balm

Lemon Grass

Lemon Verbena

Licorice sticks

Linden flowers

Lobelia leaves

Malva

Mandrake root

Mate leaves

Milk, powdered

Millet

Motherwort

Mu

Myrrh powder

Nettles

Noodles, buckwheat

Noodles, whole wheat

Orange blossoms

Papaya leaves

Passion Flower

Pennyroyal

Peppermint

Plantain

Popcorn

Pumpkin seeds

Raspberry leaves

Red clover

Red sage

Rice, brown

Rice, sweet

Rosebuds

Rose hips

Rue

Sanicle

Sarsaparilla root

Sassafras bark

Self-heal

Sesame seeds

Skullcap

Slippery Elm bark, powdered

Soybeans

Spearmint

Spikenard

Star Anise

Strawberry leaves

Sunflower seeds

Tansy

Valerian root

Violet leaves

White Oak bark

White Pine bark

Wild Cherry bark

Wintergreen

Witch Hazel

Yarrow

OLD TOWN NATURAL FOODS (Cont'd)

A good offering of quality natural foods such as grains, flours, cereals and herbs. They also have a selection of herbal soaps and shampoos. Old Town concentrates on bulk orders, encouraging formation of food co-ops, but will also sell small orders.

Price list free, but they ask that you send a stamp

OMAHA STEAKS INTERNATIONAL
4400 S. 96th St.
Omaha, Neb. 68127

CONNOISSEURS' CORNER

PRODUCTS:

Bacon, smoked	Ham, dry cured
Caviar, beluga	Lamb chops
Chateaubriand	Lobsters/lobster products
Chicken cordon bleau	Pheasant
Cornish game hen	Pork chops
Crabs/crab products	Quail
Duck a l'orange	Salmon/salmon products

60

Shrimp/shrimp products
Snapper, red
Steak:
  filet mignon
  porterhouse
  rib

sirloin
strip
T-bone
Turkey, smoked
Veal

Omaha Steaks International sells frozen beaf steaks and
other gourmet foods to mail order customers throughout
the country. They claim it's possible to order from anywhere
in the country and within three weeks receive your frozen
food in excellent condition. It is impossible to browse through
this company's catalog without going into hunger shock. The
beautifully printed color catalog can actually make you feel
hungry even if you've just finished an eight course meal.
Besides a great variety of steaks, chops and roasts, various
combination gift orders are offered. A gourmet section in the
back of the catalog offers frozen partially-prepared delights
such as Breast of Chicken Cordon Bleau, Duck a l'orange,
Coq au vin, etc. Here is a description of their Chicken
Wellington: "Tender, young breast of chicken coated with
pate, then wrapped in puff pastry to serve with Madeira
Sauce. The layer of pate is made of duck, chicken and pork,
plus eggs, shallots, tomato puree and mushrooms. Bakes in
30 minutes."

23 page color catalog free

WACHTERS' ORGANIC SEA PRODUCTS CORP.
1550 Rollins Road
Burlingame, Ca. 94010

PRODUCTS:

Food supplements/vitamins

Since 1932, Wachters' has been developing organic food
supplements and other products derived from seaweed and

other sea vegetation. Besides food supplements, vitamins and concentrated, high-protein emergency food packs, their products include cosmetics, fertilizers and livestock feed supplements.

Brochures and price list free

ORIENTAL COUNTRY STORE
12 Mott St.
New York, N.Y. 10013

PRODUCTS:

Abalone

Bamboo shoots

Bean curd

Fortune cookies

Ginger

Kumquats

Licorice root

Lychee nuts

Mushrooms, dried (Chinese)

Oyster sauce

Peanuts, raw

Sesame oil

Bean sauce

Egg, thousand year

Five spice powder

Sesame paste

Sesame seeds

Shark's fin

Shrimp chips   Shrimp

Shrimp/shrimp products

Soy sauce

Squid

Water chestnuts

The Oriental Country Store stocks a rather long line of Chinese and other items. Many of their offerings are quite unique, such as gingconut, szechuan peppercorn and shao hsing wine. In addition, they carry oriental cooking utensils, leaving the lover of these foods with no excuse but to enjoy them.

Catalog free

OZARK MOUNTAIN SMOKE HOUSE, INC.
P.O. Box 37
Farmington, Ark. 72730

PRODUCTS:

Bacon, smoked
Canadian bacon
Chicken, smoked
Ham, smoked
Sausage, smoked
Turkey, smoked

For years, gourmets have enjoyed the hickory smoked, sugar cured flavor of hams, bacon, sausage and other fine meats from the Ozark Mountains. The people at Ozark Mountain Smoke House mix their own cures and add no water to the products. In addition to their mail order services, they have four retail outlets in Arkansas and one soon to be opened in Tulsa, Oklahoma.

Colorful catalog free

THE PACKING SHED
P.O. Box 11
Weyers Cave, Va. 24486

PRODUCTS:

Peanuts, salted

This is a small company with only one product, salted **peanuts**. This traditional Tidewater Virginia delicacy is cooked in small batches, salted, and completely free of additives and preservatives. They are shelled, water blanched, cooked in oil, salted, and packed in tins for all y'all peanut lovers.

Brochure free

PAPRIKAS WEISS IMPORTER
1546 2nd Ave.
New York, N.Y. 10028

PRODUCTS:

Afrika Tanzanian coffee
Allspice
Almonds
Almond paste
Almond pudding powder
Althea root
Anchovies
Anchovy paste
Anise flavoring
Anise seed
Apple pie seasoning
Apricot butter
Apricot flavoring
Apricot jam
Apricot-pistachio delight
Arrowroot
Asparagus
Baby carrots
Baby lima beans
Baclava pastry
Baking chocolate
Baking powder
Barbeque seasoning
Barley, white
Basil
Bay leaves
Bearnaise sauce
Beef bourguignonne
Beef consomme
Beef cubes
Beef flavor base
Beef stew
Beef Stroganoff

Bitter flavoring
Bitter kernels
Bitter orange marmalade
Blackberry flavoring
Blackberry jam
Black cherry jam
Black currants
Black currant jam
Black eyed peas
Black Indian tea
Black pepper
Black turtle beans
Black walnut
Bowties, pasta
Bouquet garni
Brazillian santos coffee
Brazil nuts
Breast tea
Brown rice
Bryndza cheese
Buchette toast
Budapest ham
Buckwheat flour
Buckwheat groats

64

Bulgar

Burnt almonds

Cake layers, unfilled

Cake & pastry fillings

Calf's foot jelly

Calif. small white beans

Candied apricots in brandy

Candied baby chestnuts in cognac

Candied pears in pear liqueur

Candy cordials

Candy carrots

Candy corn

Caramel pudding powder

Caraway

Caraway flavoring

Cardamon

Cashew rocks

Cashews

Celery seasoning

Celery seed

Celery soup mix

Century herb

Ceylon breakfast tea

Chamomile tea

Charcoal seasoning salt

Cherries, candied, green

Cherries, candied, red

Cherries in cherry liqueur

Cherry flavoring

Chervil

Chestnut flour

Chestnut puree

Chestnut stuffing

Chicken consomme

Chicken cubes

Chicken noodle soup mix

Chicken style soup base

Chick peas

Chilies, whole

Chili peppers

Chili powder

China black tea

China oolong tea

China restaurant tea

Chives

Chocolate almonds

Chocolate filberts

Chocolate mocha beans

Chocolate oranges

Chocolate pastilles

Chocolate peanuts

Chocolate pudding powder

Chocolate pudding w/almonds

Chocolate raisins

Chocolate sprinkles

Christmas cremes

Chrysanthemum crystals

Chunmee green tea

Cinnamon

Citron, candied

Cloves

Cocoa almonds

Cocoa flavoring

Coconut flavoring

Colombian medellin coffee

Colored sugar shots

Consomme Celestine soup mix

Coriander

Corned beef and cabbage

Corn-on-cob seasoning

Cracked wheat cereal

Cream of tartar

Cream pudding powder

Creme de menthe flavoring

Creole seasoning

Crushed corn

Crystal sugar

Crystalized Canton ginger

Crystalized decorator flowers

Cumin seed

Curry

Curry sauce mix

Danish marzipan

Darjeeling gold tip tea

Deer goulash

Deluxe couscous

Dill

Dobosh torte

Dried mushrooms

Dried plums in armagnac

Dutch gaufrette wafers

Earl Grey tea

Egg barley pasta

Egg color

Egg noodle squares

Egg shell noodle soup mix

Elbow macaroni

Elderberry jelly

Elder flowers

Endives

English breakfast tea

English-style mustard

Famillia

Farina

Fennel seed

Fennel seed tea

Filled cake layers

Filled chocolates   filled

Fish soup

Flageolet beans

Flax seed

Fenugreek seed

Formosa oolong tea

Franck's chicory coffee

French roast coffee

French-style clarified butter

Fried chicken seasoning

Fried hare

Fruit of rose jam

Fruit soup mix

Foie gras aux naturel

"Gala" chocolate pudding
    powder

Garlic

Gefilte fish

German decaffienated coffee

German mint tea

German peppermints

German smoked ham

German-style spaetzle

Ginger

Gingerbread spice

Ginger marmalade

Ginger preserves

Golden almonds

Golden rice seasoning

Gooseberry jam

Gouda cheese crispies

Grape leaves

Great northern beans

Green coffee, unroasted

Green lentils

Green pea soup mix

Guatamalan antique coffee

Gumbo file

"Gustin" corn starch

Hamburger seasoning

Haricots verts

Hazel nuts

Heather honey

Hickory smoke salt

Hip fruit

Hirschonsalz

Hollandaise sauce mix

Honey bread

Honey cake

Honey candy

Horseradish

Horehound tea

Hungarian bacon

Hungarian bee honey

Hungarian blend coffee

Hungarian chamomile tea

Hunter sauce mix

Ice cream powder

Idaho red small beans

Imported gherkins

India wafers

Irish breakfast tea

Irish fruit cake

Irish oatmeal

Italian dried chestnuts

Italian espresso

Italian herb blend

Italian rice soup mix

Jamaica blue mountain coffee

Jasmine tea

Jordan almonds

Juniper berries

Juniper berry jam

Juniper flavoring

Kam Wo (herb tea)

Kasha

Keemun black tea

Kona coffee

Lapsang souchong tea

Lavender flowers

Leek soup mix

Lemon peel

Lemon peel, candied

Lemon pudding powder

Licorice drops

Licorice root

Lima beans

Linden honey

Linzer tarts

Liver dumpling soup mix

Lung Ching green dragon tea

Mace

Maggi spaetzle

Malt candy

Malt coffee

Majoram

Mandarin orange slices in kirsch

"Mandella" pudding powder

Marron glaces

Marzipan bars

Meat ball seasoning

Meat tenderizer

Millet seeds

Mimosa oolong tea

Mint

Mint plas candy

Mocha java

Mozartkugeln

Mugwort

Mung beans

Mushroom powder

Mushroom sauce mix

Mushrooms, mixed

Mushroom soup mix

Mustard seed

Newberry seasoning

Nutmeg

Onion flakes

Onion powder

Onions, mixed

Onion soup and dip mix

Orange flavoring

Orange flower essence

Orange peel

Orange peel, candied

Orange pekoe tea

Orange slices

Orange spice tea

Oregano

Oriental jasmine tea

Ostypka

Oxtail consomme

Oxtail soup mix

Pancake and waffle mix

Paprika

Paprika bacon

Parenyica cheese

Parsley flakes

Patchouly

Pate de foie gras

Patko

Pea beans

Pear flavoring

Pecans

Peperonata

Pepper, cayenne

Pepper, creole

Pepper, red

Pepper, white

Peppercorns

Peppermint leaves

Petite pois

Pickled walnuts in syrup

Pickling spice

Pigeon peas

Pignolias

Pineapple, candied

Pine honey

Pink beans

Pinto beans

Pistachios

Pizza seasoning

Poivre aromatique

Poppy seed

Poppy seed filling

Pork goulash

Potash

Potato dumpling mix

Potato flour

Potato pancake mix

Potato soup mix

Potato sugar candy

Poultry seasoning

Pound cake flavor

Powdered gelatin

Preiselbeeren jam

Preserved apples

Preserved apricots

Preserved cherry apples

Preserved peaches

Preserved red dates

Prune butter

Prune flavoring

Pumpernickel bread

Pumpernickel bread mix

Pumpkin pie spice

Puree de foie w/truffles

Quince jam

Rainbow torte

Raspberry drops

Raspberry flavoring

Raspberry jam

Raspberry pudding powder

Ratatouille

Rate Grutze pudding powder

Ravioli with meat

Red cherry jam

Red currant jam

Red kidney beans

Red lentils

Rendered goose fat

Rice flour

Roast lamb seasoning

Roast meat seasoning

Roman beans

Rose hips

Rosemary

Rosemary leaves

Rose petals in syrup

Rose water

Roulade

Rum beans candy

Rum flavored chocolate bottles

Rum flavoring

Rum torte

Russian samovar tea

Rye bread

Rye flavoring

Sacher torte

Saffron

Sage

Sage leaves

Salad dressing seasoning

Salami, Hungarian

Salsify

Salt, crystal

Sassafras tea

Sausage, Hungarian

Sausage with saurkraut

Savory

Scotch-style oatmeal

Seafood seasoning

Seasoning, cracked pepper

Seasoning salt

Semolina

Sesame seed

Shallots

Shell noodles

Shredded coconut

Sicilian lemon drops

Silver shots

Smoked goose pate

Smyrna figs

Solid milk chocolate

Soup noodles

Sour cherries in syrup

Sour cherry flavoring

Sour cherry jam

Sour fruit slices

Sour salt

Soy beans

Soy flour

Spearmint tea

Spice cake spice
Split green peas
Split yellow peas
Stalks of celery
Steak and kidney pie
Steak seasoning, garlic
Steel cut oatmeal
St. John's bread
Stomach bitters
Stone mushrooms
Strasbourg pate maison w/truffles
Strawberry jam
Strawberry pudding powder
Stuffed cabbage
Stuffed green peppers
Stuffed vine leaves
Summer savory
Swabian egg spaetzle
Sweet pepper flakes
Swiss chocolate bars
Swiss plum jam
Swiss syrups
"Szerencs" chocolates
Tapioca, pearl
Tarragon
Tea biscuits
Tecrine Bordelaise
Thyme
Tilia flowers
Tripe
Truffles
Turkish Chiveci
Turkish coffee
Turkish delight
Turkish egg plant
Turmeric

Valerian root
Vanilla beans
Vanilla flavoring
Vanilla sauce powder
Vanillin sugar
Venison filets
Venison with mushrooms
Vermicelli soup mix
Vichysoisse soup mix
Vienna Neapolitano
Viennese ladyfingers
Viennese marshmallows
Viennese roast coffee
Viennese-style mustard
Wafer papers
Walnut leaves
Walnut oil
Walnuts
Wheat germ
Wheat pilaf
White asparagus
White gelatin sheets
White ice cap chocolate
White raisins
White rice
White sauce mix
Whole chestnuts in brine
Whole rye flour
Whole wheat flour
Wild black currant syrup
Wild boar goulash
Wild elderberry syrup
Wild fruit of rose syrup
Wild gooseberry syrup
Wild marello cherries in syrup
Wild mushrooms

Wild raspberry syrup
Wild red currant syrup
Wild rice
Wild sour cherry syrup
Wild strawberries in syrup

Wild strawberry syrup
Woodruff
Yellow cornmeal
Yingteh black tea
Zen green tea

There is nothing quite like Paprikas Weiss Importer. This mail-order gourmet shop probably has the largest selection of spices, condiments, teas, coffees and other delicacies of any company in this book. Their not-too-easy-to-use catalog is crammed with a staggering number of imported foods and cookwares. With an obvious leaning toward "middle" European tastes, Paprikas Weiss manages to be the best "continental" food source in the country. They carry a great many items utterly unavailable anywhere else. The above list speaks for itself.

Illustrated catalog with supplements, $1.00 annual subscription

PAVONE RANCH
Rt. 4, Box 472-P
Escondido, Calif. 92025

PRODUCTS:

Almonds
Oranges, navel
Oranges, Valencia

Tangelos
Tangerines

Their grove has been organic from the start, and they use no chemicals or pesticides, substituting lady bugs and mantises for pest control. All fruit is tree ripened and picked to each individual order.

Catalog free

PEPPERIDGE FARM MAIL ORDER COMPANY
P.O. Box 119
Heritage Park, Clinton, Conn. 06413

PRODUCTS:

Bacon, smoked
Canadian bacon
Cheese, cheddar
Cheese spread
Chocolates, filled
Fruitcake
Fruit spreads
Honey, blended
Maple syrup
Nuts, mixed
Peanuts, roasted
Soups, fruit
Steak, filet mignon
Steak, strip
Tea, China
Turkey, smoked

Their catalog contains both gourmet and old-fashioned American food products, from green turtle soup to pure Vermont maple syrup, from exquisite Godiva chocolates to old-fashioned fruitcake with no artificial preservatives or colors. Many of the products, which are delivered anywhere in the continental United States, are packed in reusable wooden containers such as maple buckets, old-fashioned pie and cake baskets, carpenter's boxes, etc. All products are completely guaranteed by Pepperidge Farm. They offer three gift plans: one for three months, the second for five months, and the third for seven months.

Catalog free

PERMA-PAK, INC.
40 E. 2430 South
Salt Lake City, Utah 84115

PRODUCTS:

Camping/trail foods

With the growing interest in backpacking and "roughing it" has arisen a need for foods that are compact and non-perishable. Perma-Pak has risen to the occasion and offers a line of foods that are ideal for carrying on ventures into the wild. These foods are also ideally suited for storage at home for emergency provisions.

Catalog free

PLANTATION ACRES
515 Plantation Rd.
Merritt Island, Fla. 32952

PRODUCTS:

Lychee nuts

This is mainly a wholesale house plant nursery. They have a large lychee grove and usually have dried fruit for sale. The fruit is, by necessity, shipped by air for the most expedient delivery.

PLUMRIDGE
33 E. 61st St.
New York, N.Y. 10021

PRODUCTS:

Almonds
Candy:
   caramel   licorice
   jelly   mint

Coffee beans
Pecans
Raspberries

Plumridge specializes in unique gift packages such as cabinets with each tray filled with a different confection, and their Italian wine carrier filled to order with fine sweets. How about a gingham bean bag filled with jelly beans? Even after enjoying the last mint or spiced pecan, the packages are sure to continue to be used for storage or decorating.

Price list free

PRIESTER'S PECANS
227 Old Fort Dr.
P.O. Drawer B
Fort Deposit, Ala. 36032

PRODUCTS:

Dates, pecan stuffed
Fruitcake
Fudge, pecan
Pecan brittle
Pecans
Pralines

In the 38 years they have been in operation, Priester's has certainly found a lot of ways to prepare pecans. Whether as plain old pecans or mixed with the finest glace cherries, candied pineapples, luscious dates and sun-ripened raisins into a delicious fruitcake, this southern treat is bound to please. Their pecan candies, confections and fruitcakes are hand made in small batches to allow strict quality control.

Colorful 32 page catalog free

RITCHIE BROS.
37 Watergate
Rothesay, Isle-of-Bute
Scotland

PRODUCTS:

Salmon/salmon products

Scottish salmon smoked and cured on the Isle-of-Bute,
Scotland, and dispatched to all parts of the world by air
mail. They will enclose cards when requested to do so, and
will forward gifts to customers' friends. Their smoked salmon
has a very delicate flavor, thanks to the secret family formula
they use. Their company is a four-person, family affair. They
obtain their salmon from the rivers of the highlands of
Scotland.

ROCKY HOLLOW HERB FARM
R.D. 2, Box 215
Lake Wallkill Rd.
Sussex, N.J. 07461

PRODUCTS:

Alfalfa
Allspice
Almond meal
Almonds
Angelica root
Anise seed
Apple rings
Apricots
Arrowroot
Asafoetida
Azuki beans
Balm of Gilead buds   Gilead
Bananas, dried
Barley
Basil, sweet green

Yarrow

Bay leaves	Chili peppers
Bedstraw	Chives
Benzoin	Cinnamon
Bergamot	Clover blossoms, red
Betel nuts	Cloves
Blackberry leaves	Colonial tea
Black Cohosh	Coltsfoot
Black-eyed peas	Comfrey root
Blessed Thistle	Coriander seeds
Boneset	Couscous
Borage leaves	Cranesbill root
Brazil nuts	Cumin seeds
Broom tops	Currants, dried
Buckwheat flour	Curry
Buchi leaves	Damiana
Bulgar	Dandelion leaves
Burdock root	Dates, unpitted
Calendula flowers	Dill seed
Calumus root	Dill weed
Capiscum	Dittany of Crete
Caraway seeds, black	Elder bark
Caraway seeds, brown	Elder flowers
Cardamon seeds, green	Elecampane root
Carob beans	Eucalyptus
Carrots, seed	Everlasting
Cashews	Eyebright
Catnip	Fennel seed
Celery seeds	Fenugreek leaves
Centaury Herb	Figs
Chamomile	Flax seeds
Chaparral	Fo-Ti-Tieng
Cherries, bing, dried	Garlic
Chervil	Gentian root
Chestnuts	Ginger
Chick peas	Ginseng
Chicory root	Gold Thread

Goldenrod

Goldenseal root

Gotu Kola

Gram, black African

Granola

Ground Ivy

Gum Arabic

Hawthorne berries

Hazelnuts

Henna

Hickory bark

High John the Conqueror root

Hollyhock

Horehound

Horsetail Grass

Huckleberry

Hyssop

Iceland Moss

Irish Moss

Jersey Tea root

Juniper berries

Kelp

Kittatiny Tea

Lady's Mantle

Lavender flowers

Lemon Balm

Lemon Verbena

Lentils

Licorice root

Linden

Lobelia

Lotus roots

Lotus seeds

Lovely Flower Tea

Lychee nuts

Mace

Mastic

Marjoram, sweet

Millet

Mugwort

Mullien flowers

Mullien leaves

Mung beans

Mustard seed, black

Mustard seed, yellow

Nettle, stinging

Nutmeg

Oak bark, red

Onion flakes

Orange blossoms

Oregano

Orris root

Parsley

Passion Flower

Papaya

Paprika

Patchouly leaves

Pea beans

Peach kernels

Peaches, sun dried

Peanuts

Pears, sun dried

Pecans

Pennyroyal

Pepper

Peppermint

Periwinkle

Pignolias

Pineapple

Pinto beans

Pistachios

Pomegranate seeds

Poppy flowers, red

Poppy seeds, blue

Prunes, sun dried

Pumpkin seeds

Queen of the Meadow

Raisins

Raspberry leaves, red

Raspberry leaves, wild

Rice, brown

Rolled oat flakes

Rosebuds

Rose hips

Rosemary

Rue

Rye berries

Safflowers

Saffron

Sage

Sarsaparilla root

Sanicle leaves

Sassafras

Savory, summer

Saw Palmetto berries

Sesame seeds, black

Sesame seeds, white

Seven herb tea

Skullcap

Slippery Elm bark

Sloe berries

Southernwood

Soy beans

Spearmint

Spice Bush berries

Spice Bush twigs

Split peas

Squaw Tea

Star Anise

Stillingia root

St. John's Wort

Strawberry leaves

Sumac berries

Sunflower seeds

Sweet Bettina tea

Tansy

Tarragon

Thyme

Tonka beans

Trappers Tea

Turmeric

Uva Ursi

Valerian root

Valley Tea

Vanilla beans

Vervain

Walnuts

Wheat germ

Whole wheat berries

Witch Hazel bark

Woodruff

Wormwood

Wormwood, Roman

Yarrow flowers

Yellow Dock root

Yerba Mate

Yerba Santa

As they describe it themselves, Rocky Hollow Herb Farm is located in the foothills of the Kittatinny Mountains, on

Pochuck Mountain, at the base of Waywayanda Mountain, on the edge of the rich, fertile Wallkill River Valley. In addition to imported spices and herbs, they also supply many wild herbs, berries and fruits which grow on their abundant acreage. They have an extensive offering of essential oils, herbal baths and pot pourri, as well as their list of herbs and spices.

H. ROTH & SON
1577 First Ave.
New York, N.Y. 10028

PRODUCTS:

Agar agar

Alfalfa

Allspice

Almond paste

Anise seed

Annatto seeds

Arrowroot

Barley

Bay leaves

Beans:

   mung

   black turtle

   lima

Beeswax

Beifuss (mugwort)

Bishopswort/Flohblume (Wood
   Betony)

Black Indian root

Black pepper

Black walnut hulls

Black walnut leaves

Blue mallow flower (Malve)

Blue stone

Bohnenkraut

Boldo leaf

Buckwheat

Buchu (Gollerstrauch)

Cake decorations:

   edible flowers

   edible leaves

Capers

Caraway seed

Cardamon

Catnip

Cayenne pepper

Celery salt

Celery seed

Chamomile

Cherries, dried

Cherry stems, dried
Chervil
Chestnuts
Chili peppers
Chili powder
Chocolate:
   coffee beans
   Droste's
   lentils
   mint
   rings
   shots
Chocolate, summer coating:
   brown
   gr. pink
   white
Cinnamon
Cinnamon hearts
Cloves
Coffee royals
Coriander
Corn meal
Corn starch
Cream stabilizer   stabilizer
Creme of tartar
Crystal sugar:
   green
   orange
   pink
   rainbow
   red
   violet
   white
   yellow
Crystallized anise seed
Crystallized coriander seed

Crystallized cumin seed
Crystallized lavender
Crystallized lilacs
Crystallized mimosa
Crystallized mint leaves
Crystallized rose petals
Crystallized roses
Crystallized violets
Cumin seed
Curry powder
Dandelion root
Dandelion leaves
Dill, cut
Dill, dried
Dill seed
Egg drops
Egg noodles
Eibish blatter (marshmallow leaves)
Eibish blumen (marshmallow
   flowers)
Eibish wurzel (marshmallow root)
Elderberry blossom
"Elisen" Lebkuchen
Elm bark (slabs)
Essences:
   anisette
   apricot
   arrac
   banana
   bitter almond
   bittere topfer
   blackberry
   bourbon
   brandy
   cherry
   creme de cacao

creme de menthe
curacao
gin
grenadine
kaiserbirne
kummel
lemon
lingonberry
maple
maraschino
mocha
peach
pistachio
raspberry
root beer
rum
rye
scotch
slivowitz
stega
strawberry
vanilla
vermouth
waldmeister
walnut

Eucalyptus leaves
Fancy raspberries
Farhinha de Mandioca
Farina
Fenugreek
Fenugreek seed
Fennel seeds
Fishes, candy
Flax seed
Food colors

Flour:
  chestnut
  chick pea
  potato
  pumpernickel
  rice
  rye
  soya bean
  whole wheat
French flageolets
French peppermints
Fruit, dried candied
Garlic:
  granulated
  powder
  salt
Gelatin
Ginger
Gingerbread hearts
Ginger root
goose liver   Goose liver
Goulash spice mix
Gumbo file
Gum drops
Hagenbutten
Hats, candy
Hawthorne berries
Hazlenut crunch
Herring, Bismark
Herring, fried
Herrings in aspic
Hirschhornsalz
Hominy grits
Honey:
  Bavarian pine

Central American coffee
blossom
Dutch clover
Dutch heather
French lavender
French rosemary
German linden
German pinewood
Greek hymetius
Hungarian acacia
Israeli kosher
Spanish rosemary
Honey bread
Honey cake
Honey filled drops
Hops
Horehound
Horehound cough drops
Hulled wheat
Irish coffee-flavored chocolate
bars
Irish Moss
Lekvar jams & preserves
Juniper berries
Knotgrass
Lavender flowers (French)
Lebkuchen/Honey cake spice
Lemon Balm
Lemon Verbena
Lentils
Licorice chips
Licorice root
Liquid colors
Lyle's golden syrup
Mace
Malve

Marjoram
Marzipan
Meringue powder, deluxe
Millet seed
Mixed spices (pickling)
Mustard seed
Molasses, West Indian
Nonpariel seeds
Nuts:
    almonds
    almonds, paper shell
    bitter kernels
    Brazil nuts
    coconut flakes
    coconut, shredded
    filberts
    hazelnuts
    peanuts
    pecans
    pine nuts
    pistachios
    walnuts
    walnuts, paper shell
Nutmeg
Onion flakes
Onion powder
Onion salt
Orange peel
Oregano
Orris root
Parsley flakes
Pastilles
Patchouli

Peas:

    chick

    green

    yellow

Peacock eggs

Pectin

Peppermint drops

Peppermint ice candy

Piping gel

Pischinger-style wafer sheets

Pleurisy Root

Popcorn

Potash

Potato marzipan

Potato starch

Potato sugar candy

Poultry seasoning

Pumpkin seeds

Quatre epices (French spice mix)

Raspberries, dried

Red clover tops

Rice:

    Basmatti

    Italian

    Texas Patina

    wild

    yellow

Rice paper wafer sheets

Rock candy

Rollmops

Rosebuds

Rose hips

Rosemary

Rose water

Rum beans

Rum truffle

Russian black caraway

Sachet

Saffron

Sage

Sago

Salad herb mix

Salicyl

Saltpeter

Sardines

Sassafras bark

Sassafras root

Savory

Scouring Rush herb

Sea salt

Senna

Sesame seeds

Shots:

    blue

    gold

    red

    silver

Slippery Elm

Sour drops

Sour salt

Spaetzle

Spearmint leaves

Spice drops

Spice gum drops

Spices, Indonesian:

    boemboe

    daon salam

    daon serek

    djerek

    gulai

    kentjur

laos

poeroet

Star Anise

Steel cut oats

St. John's Bread

Strudel flour

Sumac

Sunflower seeds

Sweet Basil

Sweet Root

Szechuan pepper

Tamarind

Tapioca

Tarragon

Teas:

   breast

   centaury

   Ceylon Russian

   darjeeling

   Earl Grey

   English breakfast

   eyebright

   Formosa oolong

   gunpowder

   Imported Kneipp teas:

      Abfuehr

      Alvas

      Aranyer

      Arterien

      Asthma

      Asztma

      Baerentrauben

      Baldrian

      Blutreinigung

      Csaladi Egeszseg

      Diet

Enhye Hashajto

Epe es Maj

Epeko

Er

Familien Gesundheit

Flatulenz

Galle/Leber

Gaz

Gyomor

Haemorhoide

Harnsaeure

Herz

Husten

Ideg

Kieselsaeure

Kohoges

Magen

Nerven

Nieven/Blaser

Rheuma

Schlaf

Schlankheit

Sniv

Sovanyito

Vertisztito

Vese/Holyag

Vizele Hajto

Vizeletsau

Wassertreibend

jasmine

Kamillen

lapsang souchong

lekvar

linden

meng cha

panfried green

peppermint	Vanilla beans
raspberry leaf	Wermuth
Taiwan keemun	Wheat for soup
Yerba Mate	Wheat germ
Thyme	Wheat pilaf
Tonka beans	White Oblatten
Truffles	White pepper
Turmeric	Woodruff
Turtle seasoning	Yarrow
Valerian root	

This is a continental bazaar of gourmet foods and spices. The Roth family make frequent trips to the continent to bring the rare, the unique, the fanciful treats from all over the world. While browsing through their catalog, it is hard to resist the temptation to try some new delicacy or to indulge in an old favorite. They also have a rather extensive list of utensils and cookbooks

SAHADI IMPORTING CO.
187-189 Atlantic Ave.
Brooklyn, N.Y. 11201

PRODUCTS:

Allspice	
Almonds	
Almonds, sugar coated	
Almond syrup	
Amsure powder	Apricot preserves
Anchovies	Apricots, glazed
Aniseed	Apricot sheets, pressed
Aniseed, sugar coated	Apricots, imported natural
Apples, dried	Artichokes
Apricot candy squares	Baba Ghannouj dip
Apricot jam	Baby okra

Baklawa, pistachio filled

Baklawa, walnut filled

Basterma

Bay leaves

Besmati rice

Black olives

Bonita fillet

Braided cheese

Bulgar

Burma

Butter for cooking

California dates

Caraway

Cardamon seeds, black

Carob syrup

Cashew nuts

Chamomile

Cherry jam

Chick pea flour

Chick peas

Chick peas, roasted

Chick peas, salted

Chick peas, sugar coated

Chili pepper

Chilly pickle

Chutney pickle

Cinnamon

Citric acid

Clams, smoked

Cloves

Coconut oil

Coffee, Mid-East style, dark

Coriander seeds

Coriander, sugar coated

Couscous

Crab meat

Cumin seeds

Curry powder

Dakka (mixed spices)

Dark honey

Date jam

Dates

Dough, Baklawa

Dough, Burma

Eggplant, dried

Eggplant, pickled

Fava beans

Fennel seeds

Fennel seed, sugar coated

Fenugreek

Fig jam

Figs

Figs, imported natural

Filberts

Fish jellies

Foul Mudammas

Fruit rolls

Garbit

Garlic

Ginger

Glazed apricot hard candy

Glazed Australian figs

Glazed Australian quince

Gram Dall

Grape delight

Grape molasses

Greek cheese

Greek delight, with almonds

Green Chinese beans

Green olives

Guava juice

Guava shells in syrup

Halawa:

  chocolate

  marble

  plain

  vanilla

  with nuts

  with pistachio

Halloum cheese

Hard candy

Harissa

Hearts of palm

Henna

Honey, pure

Houmous-Bi-Tahini

Indian nuts

Iranian split apricots

Kahu Foul Mudammas

Kama (truffles)

Kashkawan cheese

Katayif, almond filled

Kefolitiri cheese

Khowlanjan

Koul Weshkour, nut filled

Lakerda (pickled fish)

Lebanese green cardamon

Lebanese Tahini

Lemon pickle

Lentil pilaf

Lentils

Lentil soup

Lentils, red split

Licorice chips

Lime pickle

Lupini

Lychees in syrup

Macadamia nuts

Mackerel fillet

Mahlab

Marjoram

Mamoul:

  date filled

  pistachio filled

  walnut filled

Mango juice

Mango pickle

Mango, sliced, in syrup

Mastic gum

Mastic jam

Melon seeds

Minestrone soup

Mint

Mint lentils

Mira lemon pickle

Mixed green olives & peppers

Mixed nuts

Mixed spices for curry

Mixed vegetables

Mizitri cheese

Mloukhiyeh

Moghrabiyeh

Mong Dall

Mushrooms

Mustard oil

Natural brown rice

Natural raisins

Nectarines, dried

Nutmeg

Okra

Okra with tomatoes

Olive oil

Orange blossom water

Orange marmalade

Oysters, smoked

Pappadums

Paprika

Pawa (rice flakes)

Peaches, dried

Peaches, glazed

Pears, dried

Pears, glazed

Peppers, pickled

Plum jam

Pignolia nuts

Pineapple, imported, sun-dried

Pistachio fingers

Pistachio nuts

Pistachios, sugar coated

Pomegranate syrup

Poppy seeds

Prunes, imported natural

Pumpkin seeds

Quince jam

Rahat Locoum

Raisins

Raspberry jellies

Red hot pepper

Rice, brown

Rice flour

Rice pilaf

Rock candy

Rock lobster

Rosa marina

Rosemary leaves

Rose petal jam

Rose water

Saffron

Salad oil

Salonica beans, white

Sahlab

Sardines

Semolina

Sesame candy squares

Sesame oil (Seerij)

Shrimps

Silver candy decorations

Soap root

Soujouk

Sour cherry jam

Squash

Squid

St. John's Bread

Strawberry jam

Stuffed eggplant

Stuffed peppers

Stuffed vine leaves

Sumac

Sunflower seeds

Syrian bread

Syrian cheese

Tahini (crushed sesame) oil

Tamarind, dry seedless

Tamarind syrup

Tarama (fish roe)

Toor Dall

Trigona

Turkish delight

Turkish delight with pistachio

Turkish Halawa

Turkish leek

Turnips, pickled

Turmeric

Urad Dall

Vanillin powder

Vermicelli

SAHADI IMPORTING CO. (Cont'd)

Walnuts, shelled
Wheat, hulled
Wheat pilaf
White truffles

Whole wheat
Whole wheat flour
Wine vinegar
Zaatar

This company offers an extremely large assortment of imported cereals, beans, candies, preserves, pastries, nuts, seeds, dried fruits, olives, etc. Their selection is from all over the world, but they favor near eastern specialties, with such exotica as Mazahr (orange blossom water) from Beirut and Mloukhiyeh (cut green leaves cooked in brine) from Damascus. The only things missing in their catalog are belly dancers.

Catalog free, $15.00 minimum order

SALTWATER FARM
Varrell Lane
York Harbor, Me. 03911

PRODUCTS:

Clams/clam products
Crabs/crab products
Fish chowder
Lobsters/lobster products
Salmon/salmon products

Shrimp/shrimp products
Snapper, red
Steaks, filet mignon
Steaks, sirloin

Saltwater Farm specializes in the shipment of live lobsters and clams from the coast of Maine. They also have a good selection of other seafood products and steaks.

Colorful 16 page catalog free

SCHALLER & WEBER, INC.
22-25 46th St.
Long Island City, N.Y. 11105

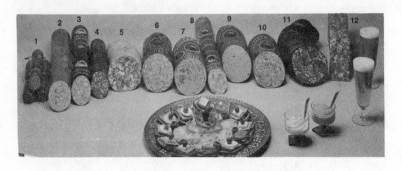

PRODUCTS:

Bacon, smoked

Blood and tongue

Bockwurst

Bologna

Braunschweiger

Cervelat

Frankfurters

Ham, smoked

Knackwurst

Salami

Sausage, ring

Schaller & Weber manufactures and distributes a large variety of gourmet wursts, salamis, cervelats, sausages and smoke-cured Westphalian and Black Forest hams, as well as bacon specialties made from the prize recipes of Ferdinand Schaller. They have received the highest awards from international food exhibitions and continue to provide the finest in old world meat delicacies.

Brochure free

SCHAPIRA COFFEE CO.
117 W. 10th St.
New York, N.Y.

PRODUCTS:

Coffee:	Tea:	
blends	blends	green
decaffienated	Ceylon	jasmine
Guatamala	darjeeling	lapsang souchong
Java	Earl Grey	oolong
Mexico	Formosa	
Venezuela		

Schapira offers coffees for most any taste, both distinctive imported favorites and their own mocha-Colombian blend which can be ordered in three styles: American roast, French roast, and Italian. They are one of the few companies to have Djimmah, a rare coffee from Ethiopia, with unique flavor and exquisite aroma. They also have teas from around the world, including such rarities as assam and keemun.

Price list free

SHOFFEITT PRODUCTS CORP.
420 Hudson St.
Healdsburg, Ca. 95448

PRODUCTS:

Spices/seasoners

Shoffeitt Products Corp. developed, manufactures and markets an extensive line of gourmet seasoners and salad dressing/dip mixes that are quite unique. Lemon-Garlic, Lemon-Herb and Lemon-Dill are only a few of the often exotic, always good flavors available. Many of the seasoners are completely organic, with no MSG or preservatives. These seasoners are available either singly or in gift packs ranging from four to 15 flavors, from a gaily printed cardboard box to a three-tiered walnut spice case.

Color illustrated catalog free

91

SMITHFIELD HAM PRODUCTS CO., INC.
P.O. Box 487
Smithfield, Va. 23430

PRODUCTS:

Bacon, Smithfield
Barbeque sauce
Beef barbeque
Beef stew
Brunswick stew
Chili con carne
Ham, deviled
Ham, Smithfield
Hash, beef   Pork barbeque
Horseradish   Turkey barbeque

Smithfield was part of the first colony on the south side of
the James River in Virginia. It became the first trading center
on the south side. Hams from the port of Smithfield, later
known as Smithfield hams, were among the first items used
in barter, trade and export to England and the Netherlands.
These products have been world famous for several hundred
years for their unique quality and distinctiveness.

Catalog free

STERNBERG PECAN COMPANY
P.O. Box 193
Jackson, Miss. 39205

PRODUCTS:

Pecans

Sternberg's, founded in 1938, pioneered in selling shelled
pecans by mail, after perfection of the automatic sheller
made fresh-shelled pecans available to persons outside the
relatively small area of the United States which grows the
entire world's supply of the nut. Their pecans come from the

STERNBERG PECAN CO. (Cont'd)

heart of this growing area and seldom are available elsewhere. They also publish a recipe folder which will be sent for postage and handling charge of 20¢. Payment in stamps for the folder is acceptable. The recipe folder is sent free of charge to persons ordering pecans.

Brochure free

STOCK YARDS PACKING CO., INC.
340 N. Oakley Blvd.
Chicago, Ill. 60612

PRODUCTS:

Beef, chopped	Roasts:
Canadian bacon	rib
Capons	sirloin
Chicken a la Kiev	tenderloin
Cornish game hens	Shrimp/shrimp products
Ham	Steak:
Lamb chops	filet mignon
Lamb, leg of	rib
Lobster/lobster products	sirloin
Pork chops	T-bone
	Veal

STOCKYARDS PACKING CO. (Cont'd)

The Stock Yards Packing Company has been supplying meats since 1893. One would have a hard time deciding among their many cuts of beef, pork, seafood and poultry. Perhaps a mouth-watering leg of lamb will fit the bill. Whatever the choice, it is certain to be a delight to anyone who enjoys fine meats.

Catalog free

SUGARBUSH FARM, INC.
R.F.D. 3
Woodstock, Vt. 05091

PRODUCTS:

Candy, bon bon
Candy, maple
Cheese:
   bleu
   cheddar
   hickory smoked
   Vermont
Syrup, maple

Fine Vermont cheeses and maple products, some of which would be hard to find anywhere else. Take, for example, their Green Mountain Jack, an eastern variation of the famous Monterey Jack. This is a delightful mild cheese with a quite unique flavor. For a rich, creamy cheese, try Sugarbush Farm's Stilton bleu (great in salads). All their cheeses are free from preservatives, colorings or chemicals.

Catalog free

SWANJORD HATCHERY
Balaton, Minn. 56115

PRODUCTS:

Eggs:
    duck
    goose
    sparrow

Swanjord Hatchery offers goose eggs in peewee to jumbo sizes and duck eggs, either white or blue-colored. At times they also have guinea, pheasant and other kinds of eggs. They welcome inquiries as to amounts and prices.

Price list free

SWISS CHEESE SHOPS, INC.
Hwy 69 N.
Monroe, Wisc. 53566

PRODUCTS:

Cheese:
    bleu/blue
    cheddar
    Colby
    limburger   Swiss
    muenster   Wisconsin

Wisconsin is one of the nation's leading cheese producing states and the Swiss Cheese Shops certainly show this. They have quite a list of not only Swiss but many other types, some of them rather hard to find. The garlic cheddar sounds just the thing for a wild attack of the munchies, and when it's available their smoked Swiss may just cause any gourmet to smile with pleasure. They also carry gift assortments with taste-tempting combinations of their offerings.

Catalog free

THE SWISS COLONY
1112 7th Ave.
Monroe, Wisc. 53566

PRODUCTS:

All beef log

Almond cheese roll

Almond crescent

Almond dobosh

Almond pecan logs

American cheese

American cheese, aged

Angel food

Apples

Apricot cordial cake

Apricot preserves

Australian lobster tails

Bacon

Bacon cheese roll

Banana nut cake

Beerwurst

Bel paese

Blackberry preserves

Bleu cheese

Boccine

Boneless ham roll

Boneless strip steak

Braunschweiger sausage

Brick cheese

Brick log

Butter cookies

Butter creme dobosh

Butter creme torte

Butter creme triangles

Butter mints

Butter-rum fruitcake

Butterscotch toffee

Butter toasted peanuts
Butter toffee
Canadian bacon
Candy canes
Caramel pecan wheel
Caramel nut swirl
Caraway beef
Caraway cheese
Caraway sausage
Cashews
Ceylon tea
Cha ching tea
Cheddar cheese
Cheddar club
Cheddar, sharp
Cheddar with almond logs
Cheddar with bacon
Cheddar with onion
Cheddar with pecans
Cheddar with port wine
Cheddar with sherry
Cheddar with walnuts
Cheddi, beef
Cheese 'n' meat
Cheese and salami
Cherries
Cherry-brandy snow cake roll
Cherry cordial cake
Cherry-elderberry preserves
Chicken a la Kiev
Chicken al la regal
Chicken cordon bleu
Chocolate balls
Chocolate Christmas cake
Chocolate creme wafers
Chocolate dobosh torte

Chocolate house
Chocolate mints
Chocolate pecan logs
Chocolate yule wreath
Christmas butter stollen
Christmas mints
Christmas mix candy
Cinnamon apple pancake mix
Cinnamon apple preserves
Coconut patties
Colby cheese
Comice pears
Cordial cakes
Cornish game hens
Creme de cocoa cordial cake
Creme de cocoa yule log
Creme de menthe dobosh
Creme de menthe torte
Cremo (imported spread)
Dates
Dobosh torte
Double chocolate dobosh torte
Dried fruit
Edam cheese
Edam triangles
Egg nog nut cake
English tea
English walnuts
Figs
Filbert nuts
Filet mignon
Fruitcake
Fudge nut dobosh
Fudge nut ring
Fudge nut torte
Fudge ring

Gingerbread

Gouda

Gouda, smoked

Gouda with caraway

Grapefruit

Ham

Hawaiian macadamia nuts

Hawaiian macadamia nut cake

Hickory smoked cheese

Holland ham

Imported link sausage

Jasmine tea

Kummel kase sticks

Laona bacon

Light buttermilk mix

Liqueur chocolates

Liqueur mints

Liver and bacon roll

Liver sausage

Longhorn cheddar

Macadamia nut cake

Macadamia torte

Mandarin tea

Maple nut fudge

Marshmallows

Marzipan tray

Mineola tangelo oranges

Mint honey

Mint tea

Mint toffee

Mint torte

Mixed nuts

Moisturized fruit

Mortadella

Muenster

Nutty crunch

Old world cookies

Omelet

Onion cheese balls

Oolong tea

Orange blossom honey

Orange cordial cake

Orange marmalade

Orange nut cake

Oranges

Paprika cheese

Peanuts

Pecan-cheddar wheel

Pecan cheese ball

Pecan pound cake

Pepper cheese

Petit beurre

Petits fours

Pineapple

Pistachios

Pizza

Popcorn, honey caramel

Port salut

Prime filets

Process Gruyere

Prunes

Redcoat cheddar

Rock Cornish hens

Rolled dobosh torte

Rum cordial cake

Samsoe

Satin candy

Sherry cheese roll

Sherry log roll

Smoked ring neck pheasant

Smoked turkey

Smoked turkey breast

THE SWISS COLONY (Cont'd)

Smokee triangles
Spiced cocktail almonds
Sportstex
Strawberry buds
Strawberry jam
Strawberry nut torte
Summer sausage
Swedish pancake mix
Swiss cheese

Swiss process gruyere
Swiss-O-Brick
Swiss & rye cheese
Tenderloin steak
Toffee
Vanilla pecan logs
Yachtswurst
Yule log

Specializing in gift sets of fine cheeses, hams and other delicacies, the Swiss Colony offers many unique packages. One would have to search far to find such things as Swiss Colony's pecan cheddar wheel or their ten foot sausage. Most of their goodies are imported, giving the customer a good choice of old world treats as well as the best of this continent. They also operate the Cheese Gift of the Month Plan, allowing giving to be spread across the calendar.

Colorful, interesting catalog free

THOUSAND ISLAND APIARIES
Rt. 2
Clayton, N.Y. 13624

PRODUCTS:

Honey, clover

This honey is one that has not been cooked or filtered, but warmed just enough to go through a coarse white sand strainer. All the equipment at Thousand Island Apiaries is stainless steel and the honey flows through a closed line, thereby insuring retention of flavor and food value. The honey may be had in liquid form, crystallized, or as comb honey.

Descriptive brochure free

TIMBER CREST FARMS
4791 Dry Creek Rd.
Healdsburg, Calif. 95448

PRODUCTS:

Fruit, dried

Apparently a wholesale supplier to health food outlets,
Timber Crest Farms offers dried fruits in bulk from their
farms in the fruit growing valleys of Northern California. It
may be possible for food cooperatives to obtain large orders
from them.

VICTORIA PACKING CORP.
443 E. 100th St.
Brooklyn, N.Y. 11236

PRODUCTS:

Artichokes/artichoke hearts

Basil

Bay leaves

Beans, lupini

Capers

Cauliflower/cauliflower products

Cherries, maraschino

Cinnamon

Cipollini

Cloves

Eggplant

Fennel

Garlic

Giardiniera

Mint

Mushrooms

Mustards

Olives

Oregano

Paprika

Parsley

Peaches

Pears

Pepper, black

Pepperoncini

Peppers:

    antipasto

    fried

    roasted

    stuffed

Pickles:

    dill

    kosher

    sour

    sweet

VICTORIA PACKING CORP. (Cont'd)

Pig's—
   ears
   feet
   knuckles
   snouts
   tails

Pumpkin seeds
Saurkraut
Sunflower seeds
Vinegar

Victoria Packing Corp. was established in 1929 and has since become a large supplier of condiments and spices. They import mountains of olives, peppers and other delicacies, and they have a line of pickled pork products hard to find elsewhere. Victoria also has a good list of spices and nut specialties to satisfy discriminating tastes.

Catalog 75¢

PETER AND TINA WATSON
1227 Dorset St.
South Burlington, Vt.

PRODUCTS:

Syrup, maple

There is nothing quite like real Vermont maple syrup flowing over hot cakes or waffles. This small, family-run business will send the pure, tasty syrup right to your door. They work hard to hang the buckets, gather the sap and keep the fires going, but the end result is well worth the effort. They will not only make your breakfast table an experience in maple, but will also answer inquiries about maple sugaring, its history and techniques.

Price list free

WOLF'S NECK FARM
Freeport, Me. 04032

PRODUCTS:

Beef quarters

Wolf's Neck Farm ships frozen organic beef which has been grown with no exposure to poison sprays, artificial growth stimulants, chemical fertilizers or health hazards. Each hindquarter, side or forequarter will yield a good supply of cuts and ground beef.

Catalog free

WONDER NATURAL FOODS
11711 Redwood Highway
Wonder, Ore. 97543

PRODUCTS:

Apricots
Bee pollen
Ginseng/ginseng products

Wonder Natural Foods is really two companies in one: East Earth Herbs, offering a complete line of Chinese ginseng and other compatible herbs, and Wonder Pollen Collective, which specializes in bee-collected pollen from ecologically pure areas in Canada, Spain, North America and Australia. They each have both wholesale and mail order retail sales.

Price list free

YOUNG PECAN SALES CORP.
P.O. Box 632
Florence, S.C. 29501

PRODUCTS:

   Fruitcake
   Pecans

Year around availability of high quality shelled pecans to mail order customers makes this company rather unique. Pecans are available plain or butter roasted. Young also will allow quantity discounts.

Price list free

MASTER INDEX

ABALONE
 Kam Shing Co.
 Les Echalottes
 Oriental Country Store
ABALONE in soy sauce
 Les Echalottes
ABSINTHE
 Aphrodesia
ADAM and Eve root
 Aphrodesia
AGAR-AGAR
 Aphrodesia
 Deer Valley Farm
 Kam Shing Co.
 Old Town Natural Foods
 Roth and Son
AGARBATTO
 K. Kalustyan
AGRIMONY
 Aphrodesia
 Lhasa Karmak Herb Co.

AJIMA seeds
 Aphrodesia
AJITSUKENORI
 Katagiri
AKADASHI
 Katagiri
ALFALFA
 Aphrodesia
 Lhasa Karnak Herb Co.
 Rocky Hollow Herb Farm
 Roth and Son
ALFALFA leaves
 Magic Garden Herb Co.
 Old Town Natural Foods
ALL spice
 Aphrodesia
 Empire Coffee and Tea Company
 Lhasa Karnak Herb Co.
 Magic Garden Herb Co.
 Paprikas Weiss Importer
 Rocky Hollow Herb Farm

Roth and Sons
Sahadi Import Co.
ALMOND butter
Jaffe Bros. Natural Foods
ALMOND cheese roll
The Swiss Colony
ALMOND crescent
The Swiss Colony
ALMOND meal
Rocky Hollow Herb Farm
ALMOND paste
Manganaro Foods
Paprikas Weiss Importer
Roth and Son
ALMOND pecan logs
The Swiss Colony
ALMONDS (see also Burnt
almonds)
Jaffe Bros. Natural Foods
Kakawateez, Limited
Paprikas Weiss Importer
Plumridge
Rocky Hollow Herb Farm
Sahadi Import Co.
ALMONDS, golden
Paprikas Weiss Importer
ALMONDS, Jordan
Paprikas Weiss Importer
ALMONDS, spiced cocktail
The Swiss Colony
ALMONDS, sugar coated
Sahadi Import Co.
ALOE
Aphrodesia
ALOE gum
Magic Garden Herb Co.
ALTHEA root
Aphrodesia
Paprikas Weiss Importer

ALUM root, white
Aphrodesia
AMANATTO
Katagiri
AMARETTI
Manganaro Foods
AMAZU-SHOGA
Katagiri
AMBRETTE seeds
Aphrodesia
AMSURE powder
Sahadi Import Co.
ANCHOVIES
Charlotte Charles, Inc.
Manganaro Foods
Paprikas Weiss Importer
Sahadi Import Co.
ANCHOVIES, fillets
Les Echalottes
ANCHOVIES, rolled
Les Echalottes
ANCHOVIES, salt
Manganaro Foods
ANCHOVY paste
Les Echalottes
Manganaro Foods
Paprikas Weiss Importer
ANGEL food
The Swiss Colony
ANGELICA
Aphrodesia
Lhasa Karnak Herb Co.
Magic Garden Herb Co.
Old Town Natural Foods
Rocky Hollow Herb Farm
ANGELIQUE, dried and candied
Roth and Son
ANGUILA
Manganaro Foods

ANISE (see also Star anise)
Aphrodesia
Empire Coffee and Tea Company
Lhasa Karnak Herb Co.
ANISE flavoring
Paprikas Weiss Importer
ANISE seed
Old Town Natural Foods
Paprikas Weiss Importer
Rocky Hollow Herb Farm
Roth and Son
Sahadi Import Co.
ANISE seed, sugar coated
Sahadi Import Co.
ANNATTO seeds
Aphrodesia
Roth and Sons
ANTIPASTO
Les Echalottes
ANTIPASTO, Milanese
Manganaro Foods
AONORIKO
Katagiri
AO uzumaki fu
Katagiri
APPLE butter
Charlotte Charles, Inc.
De Sousa's — The Healthians
APPLE pie seasoning
Paprikas Weiss Importer
APPLE rings
Charlotte Charles, Inc.
Rocky Hollow Herb Farm
APPLE sauce
Charlotte Charles, Inc.
Deer Valley Farm
APPLES, dried
Sahadi Import Co.
APPLES, dried and candied
Roth and Son

APPLES, fresh
Deer Valley Farm
The Swiss Colony
APPLES, McIntosh
The Forsts
APPLES, preserved
Paprikas Weiss Importer
APRICOT butter
Paprikas Weiss Importer
APRICOT candy square
Sahadi Import Co.
APRICOT cordial cake
The Swiss Colony
APRICOT flavoring
Paprikas Weiss Importer
APRICOT jam
Paprikas Weiss Importer
Sahadi Import Co.
Roth and Son
APRICOT kernels
Magic Garden Herb Co.
APRICOT-pistachio delight
Paprikas Weiss Importer
APRICOT preserves
Les Echalottes
Sahadi Import Co.
The Swiss Colony
APRICOT sheets, pressed
Sahadi Import Co.
APRICOTS
Charlotte Charles, Inc.
Old Town Natural Foods
Rocky Hollow Herb Farm
Wonder Natural Foods
APRICOTS, brandied
Paprikas Weiss Importer
APRICOTS, dried and candied
Roth and Son
APRICOTS, glazed
Sahadi Import Co.

APRICOTS, imported, natural
  Sahadi Import Co.
APRICOTS, Iranian split
  Sahadi Import Co.
APRICOTS, preserved
  Paprikas Weiss Importer
ARABIC, gum
  Aphrodesia
ARARE
  Katagiri
ARECA and catechu
  Magic Garden Herb Co.
ARNICA flowers
  Aphrodesia
ARROWROOT
  Aphrodesia
  Lhasa Katnak Herb Co.
  Paprikas Weiss Importer
  Rocky Hollow Herb Farm
  Roth and Son
ARTICHOKES/artichoke hearts
  Boggiatto Packing Co., Inc.
  Bremen House, Inc.
  Charlotte Charles, Inc.
  Les Echalottes
  Manganaro Foods
  Sahadi Import Co.
  Victoria Packing Corp.
ASAKUSANORI
  Katagiri
ASIFOETIDA
  Aphrodesia
  Rocky Hollow Herb Farm
ASIFOETIDA gum
  Magic Garden Herb Co.
ASPARAGUS
  Bremen House, Inc.
  Charlotte Charles, Inc.

Manganaro Foods
Paprikas Weiss Importer
ASPARAGUS, French
  Les Echalottes
ASPARAGUS, white
  Paprikas Weiss Importer
AVOCADOS
  All Organics, Inc.
  Jaffe Bros. Natural Foods
AVORIO
  Manganaro Foods
AZUKI
  Katagiri
AZUKI beans
  Rocky Hollow Herb Farm
BABA-Ferrara
  Manganaro Foods
BABA ghannouj dip
  Sahadi Import Co.
BABAS in rum, petit
  Les Echalottes
BACCALA
  Manganaro Foods
BACI
  Manganaro Foods
BACLAVA (see Baklawa)
BACON
  The Swiss Colony
BACON, Canadian (see Canadian
    bacon)
BACON cheese roll
  The Swiss Colony
BACON, Hungarian
  Paprikas Weiss Importer
BACON, Laona
  The Swiss Colony
BACON, paprika
  Paprikas Weiss Importer

BACON, Smithfield
  Smithfield Ham and Products
    Co., Inc.
BACON, smoked
  Amana Society
  The Forsts
  McArthur's Smokehouse, Inc.
  Omaha Steaks International
  Ozark Mountain Smoke House,
    Inc.
  Schaller and Weber, Inc.
BAHMI goreng
  Les Echalottes
BAKED beans (see Beans, baked)
BAKING chocolate
  Paprikas Weiss Importer
BAKING powders/yeast
  Deer Valley Farm
  Paprikas Weiss Importer
BAKLAWA (see also Dough for
    Baklawa)
BAKLAWA pastry
  Paprikas Weiss Importer
BAKLAWA, pistachio filled
  Sahadi Import Co.
BAKLAWA, walnut filled
  Sahadi Import Co.
BALM of Gilead
  Aphrodesia
  Lhasa Karnak Herb Co.
  Rocky Hollow Herb Farm
BALMONY herb
  Magic Garden Herb Co.
BAMBOO pickle
  Les Echalottes
BAMBOO shoots
  Kam Shing Co.
  Les Echalottes
  Oriental Country Store

BANANA nut cake
  The Swiss Colony
BANANA products
  Deer Valley Farm
BANANAS, dried
  Rocky Hollow Herb Farm
BARBEQUE, beef
  Smithfield Ham and Products
    Co., Inc.
BARBEQUE sauce
  Smithfield Ham and Products
    Co., Inc.
BARBEQUE seasoning
  Paprikas Weiss Importer
BARDANA root
  Magic Garden Herb Co.
BARLEY
  Rocky Hollow Herb Farm
  Roth and Son
BARLEY, white
  Paprikas Weiss Importer
BASIL
  Deer Valley Farm
  Lhasa Karnak Herb Co.
  Magic Garden Herb Co.
  Paprikas Weiss Importer
  Victoria Packing Corp.
BASIL, sweet
  Rocky Hollow Herb Farm
  Roth and Son
BASTERMA
  Sahadi Import Co.
BAY leaves
  Aphrodesia
  Lhasa Karnak Herb Co.
  Magic Garden Herb Co.
  Paprikas Weiss Importer
  Rocky Hollow Herb Farm
  Roth and Son
  Sahadi Import Co.

BAYBERRY bark
  Aphrodesia
  Lhasa Karnak Herb Co.
  Magic Garden Herb Co.
BAYBERRY bark powder
  Old Town Natural Foods
BEAN curd
  Oriental Country Store
BEAN threads
  Kam Shing Co.
BEANS (see also under specific
    type, e.g. Azuki beans, etc.)
BEANS, baked
  Charlotte Charles, Inc.
BEANS, black
  Aphrodesia
BEANS, black turtle
  Paprikas Weiss Importer
  Roth and Son
BEANS, California small white
  Paprikas Weiss Importer
BEANS, Chinese green
  Sahadi Import Co.
BEANS, great northern
  Paprikas Weiss Importer
BEANS, green
  Charlotte Charles, Inc.
  Deer Valley Farm
BEANS, Japanese
  Chico-San, Inc.
BEANS, lupini
  Victoria Packing Corp.
BEANS, Mexican style
  Les Echalottes
BEANS, mung
  Paprikas Weiss Importer
  Rocky Hollow Herb Farm
  Roth and Son

BEANS, pink
  Paprikas Weiss Importer
BEANS, pinto
  Deer Valley Farm
  Les Echalottes
  Old Town Natural Foods
  Paprikas Weiss Importer
  Rocky Hollow Herb Farm
BEANS, red kidney
  Charlotte Charles, Inc.
  Deer Valley Farm
  Old Town Natural Foods
  Paprikas Weiss Importer
BEANS, re-frying
  Les Echalottes
BEANS, stringless
  Les Echalottes
  Manganaro Foods
BEANS, Tonka
  Aphrodesia
  Rocky Hollow Herb Farm
  Roth and Son
BEANS, wax
  Charlotte Charles, Inc.
BEARNAISE sauce
  Les Echalottes
  Paprikas Weiss Importer
BEDSTRAW
  Rocky Hollow Herb Farm
BEE pollen
  Wonder Natural Foods
BEEF (see also Meat, Corned beef,
    Roasts and Steaks)
BEEF Bourguignonne
  Paprikas Weiss Importer
BEEF, chopped
  Stock Yards Packing Co., Inc.
BEEF consomme
  Paprikas Weiss Importer

BEEF cubes
  Paprikas Weiss Importer
BEEF flavor base
  Paprikas Weiss Importer
BEEF hash
  Deer Valley Farm
  Smithfield Ham and Products
    Co., Inc.
BEEF log
  The Swiss Colony
BEEF quarters
  Wolf's Neck Farm
BEEF stew
  Deer Valley Farm
  Paprikas Weiss Importer
  Smithfield Ham and Products
    Co., Inc.
BEEF Stroganoff
  Paprikas Weiss Importer
BEEF tongue, cooked
  Les Echalottes
BEEF with onion pie
  Les Echalottes
BEER/wine making supplies
  Bacchanalia
BEERWURST
  The Swiss Colony
BEESWAX
  Roth and Son
BEETS
  Charlotte Charles, Inc.
  Deer Valley Farm
BEL Paese
  Manganaro Foods
  The Swiss Colony
BELUGA
  Manganaro Foods
BENISHOGA
  Katagiri

BENNE (see Candy, benne)
BENZOIN
  Aphrodesia
  Rocky Hollow Herb Farm
BENZOIN, gum
  Magic Garden Herb Co.
BERBERI
  Aphrodesia
BERGAMOT
  Rocky Hollow Herb Farm
BESMATI rice
  Sahadi Import Co.
BETEL nuts
  Rocky Hollow Herb Farm
BETH root
  Magic Garden Herb Co.
BIRCH bark
  Aphrodesia
  Lhasa Karnak Herb Co.
BIRCH log
  The Swiss Colony
BIRD'S nest
  Kam Shing Co.
BISCUIT assortment
  Les Echalottes
BISCUITS, cocktail
  Manganaro Foods
BISCUITS for cheese
  Manganaro Foods
BISCUITS, Harvest Gomairi
  Katagiri
BISCUITS, Jacob's water
  Manganaro Foods
BISCUITS, sweet/shortbreads
  Bissinger's
  Charlotte Charles, Inc.
BISHOPSWORT
  Roth and Son

BISQUES (see Chowders/bisques;
    see also under specific type,
    e.g. Lobster bisque)
BISTORT
    Aphrodesia
    Magic Garden Herb Co.
BITTER flavoring
    Paprikas Weiss Importer
BITTER kernels
    Paprikas Weiss Importer
BITTERSWEET
    Magic Garden Herb Co.
BLACK cherry jam
    Paprikas Weiss Importer
BLACK cherry preserves
    Les Echalottes
BLACK currant jelly
    Les Echalottes
    Paprikas Weiss Importer
BLACK currants
    Paprikas Weiss Importer
BLACK eye peas
    Paprikas Weiss Importer
    Rocky Hollow Herb Farm
BLACK walnut hulls
    Roth and Son
BLACK walnut leaves
    Roth and Son
BLACK walnuts
    Paprikas Weiss Importer
BLACKBERRY flavoring
    Paprikas Weiss Importer
BLACKBERRY jam
    Paprikas Weiss Importer
BLACKBERRY jelly
    Les Echalottes
BLACKBERRY leaves
    Aphrodesia
    Rocky Hollow Herb Farm

BLACKBERRY preserves
    The Swiss Colony
BLADDERWRACK
    Aphrodesia
BLESSED thistle
    Magic Garden Herb Co.
    Rocky Hollow Herb Farm
BLOODROOT
    Lhasa Karnak Herb Co.
BLUE stone
    Roth and Son
BLUEBERRY leaves
    Aphrodesia
BOCCINE
    The Swiss Colony
BOCKWURST
    Schaller and Weber, Inc.
BOHNENKRAUT
    Roth and Son
BOLDO
    Aphrodesia
BOLDO leaf
    Roth and Sons
BOLOGNA
    Schaller and Weber, Inc.
BONCHIAGE
    Katagiri
BONESET
    Aphrodesia
    Rocky Hollow Herb Farm
BONITA fillet
    Sahadi Import Co.
BORAGE
    Aphrodesia
    Magic Garden Herb Co.
BORAGE leaves
    Rocky Hollow Herb Farm
BOUCHEES
    Charlotte Charles, Inc.

BOUILLABAISSE soup
  Les Echalottes
  Manganaro Foods
BOUILLON/soup flavoring
  Breman House, Inc.
  Charlotte Charles, Inc.
  Deer Valley Farm
BOUQUET garni
  Aphrodesia
  Les Echalottes
  Paprikas Weiss Importer
BOW ties, pasta
  Paprikas Weiss Importer
BRANDY cakes
  Les Echalottes
BRANDY flavor
  Les Echalottes
BRANDY sauce
  Les Echalottes
BRAUNSCHWEIGER
  The Forsts
  Schaller and Weber, Inc.
  The Swiss Colony
BRAZIL nuts
  Kakawateez, Limited
  Paprikas Weiss Importer
  Rocky Hollow Herb Farm
  The Swiss Colony
BREAD (see also under specific
    types, e.g. Pumpernickel
    bread)
BREAD, banana
  Deer Valley Farm
BREAD, brown
  Charlotte Charles, Inc.
  Deer Valley Farm
BREAD, date-nut
  Deer Valley Farm

BREAD, raisin
  Deer Valley Farm
BREAD, rye
  Breman House, Inc.
  Deer Valley Farm
  Paprikas Weiss Importer
BREAD, Syrian
  Sahadi Import Co.
BREAD, whole wheat
  Deer Valley Farm
BREADS, European
  Breman House, Inc.
BREADSTICKS
  Manganaro Foods
BRIOSCHI
  Manganaro Foods
BROOM tops
  Rocky Hollow Herb Farm
BRUNSWICK stew
  Smithfield Ham and Products
    Co., Inc.
BUCHEE
  Roth and Sons
BUCHEE leaves
  Aphrodesia
  Rocky Hollow Herb Farm
BUCHETTE toast
  Paprikas Weiss Importer
BUCKEYES
  Aphrodesia
BUCKTHORNE bark
  Aphrodesia
BUCKWHEAT flour
  Paprikas Weiss Importer
  Rocky Hollow Herb Farm
  Roth and Sons
BUGLEWEED
  Magic Garden Herb Co.

BULGAR
  Les Echalottes
  Paprikas Weiss Importer
  Rocky Hollow Herb Farm
  Sahadi Import Co.
BULLDOG sauce
  Katagiri
BULLDOG Tonkatsu sauce
  Katagiri
BUMBU nasi goreng (mixed spices
  & onions)
  Les Echalottes
BUNS, frankfurter/hamburger
  Deer Valley Farm
BUNS, maple nut
  Deer Valley Farm
BURDOCK root
  Aphrodesia
  Old Town Natural Foods
  Rocky Hollow Herb Farm
BURMA (see also Dough for burma)
  Sahadi Import Co.
BURNT almonds
  Paprikas Weiss Importer
BUTTER (see also under specific
  type, e.g. Almond butter, etc.)
BUTTER creme triangles
  The Swiss Colony
BUTTER, French-style, clarified
  Paprikas Weiss Importer
BUTTER for cooking
  Sahadi Import Co.
BUTTER mints
  The Swiss Colony
BUTTER, sesame
  Chico-San, Inc.
BUTTERMILK mix
  The Swiss Colony

BUTTERS/spreads, nut
  Deer Valley Farm
CABBAGE, stuffed
  Paprikas Weiss Importer
CACTUS flowers
  Aphrodesia
CAKE (see also under specific
  type, e.g. Fruit cake, etc.)
CAKE and pastry fillings
  Paprikas Weiss Importer
CAKE decorating—edible leaves,
  edible flowers
  Roth and Son
CAKE, egg nog nut
  The Swiss Colony
CAKE, layers, filled
  Paprikas Weiss Importer
CAKE, layers, unfilled
  Paprikas Weiss Importer
CAKES, nut
  Deer Valley Farm
CAKES, rice
  Byrd Cookie Co.
  Chico-San, Inc.
  Deer Valley Farm
CAKES, rum
  Charlotte Charles, Inc.
  Les Echalottes
  The Swiss Colony
CAKES, whole wheat
  Deer Valley Farm
CALAMARES
  Manganaro Foods
CALAMUS root
  Aphrodesia
  Old Town Natural Foods
  Rocky Hollow Herb Farm

114

CALENDULA flowers
Rocky Hollow Herb Farm
CALF'S foot jelly
Les Echalottes
Paprikas Weiss Importer
CALPIS
Katagiri
CAMOMILLE (see also Chamomile)
Empire Coffee and Tea
Company
Old Town Natural Foods
CAMPING/storage foods
Bernard Food Industries, Inc.
Chuck Wagon Foods
Perma-Pak, Inc.
CANADIAN bacon
Amana Society
The Forsts
McArthur's Smokehouse, Inc.
Ozark Mountain Smoke House,
Inc.
Stock Yards Packing Co., Inc.
The Swiss Colony
CANDY (see also under specific
type, e.g. Fudge, etc.)
CANDY, benne
Byrd Cookie Co.
CANDY, bon-bons
Bailey's of Boston, Inc.
Charlotte Charles, Inc.
Sugarbush Farm, Inc.
CANDY canes
The Swiss Colony
CANDY, caramel
Bailey's of Boston, Inc.
Charlotte Charles, Inc.
Plumridge

CANDY carrots
Paprikas Weiss Importer
CANDY cordials
Paprikas Weiss Importer
CANDY corn
Paprikas Weiss Importer
CANDY, decorating
Sahadi Import Co
CANDY fishes
Roth and Son
CANDY, French
Charlotte Charles, Inc.
CANDY, fruit
Charlotte Charles, Inc.
CANDY, golden apricot, hard
Sahadi Import Co.
CANDY gum drops
Roth and Son
CANDY, hard
Bailey's of Boston, Inc.
Sahadi Import Co.
CANDY, honey
Deer Valley Farm
Paprikas Weiss Importer
CANDY, horehound
Deer Valley Farm
CANDY, imported
Breman House, Inc.
CANDY, jelly
Bailey's of Boston, Inc.
Plumridge
CANDY, licorice
Deer Valley Farm
Plumridge
CANDY, malt
Paprikas Weiss Importer
CANDY, maple
Sugarbush Farm, Inc.

CANDY, mint
  Bailey's of Boston, Inc.
  Charlotte Charles, Inc.
  Plumridge
CANDY, mint peas
  Paprikas Weiss Importer
CANDY, nut
  Deer Valley Farm
CANDY, peppermint ice
  Roth and Sons
CANDY, potato sugar
  Paprikas Weiss Importer
  Roth and Son
CANDY, rice
  Chico-San, Inc.
CANDY, rum beans
  Paprikas Weiss Importer
CANDY, satin
  The Swiss Colony
CANDY, sesame
  Sahadi Import Co.
CANDY, slippery elm
  Deer Valley Farm
CAPERS
  Charlotte Charles, Inc.
  Roth and Son
  Victoria Packing Corp.
CAPONATINA
  Manganaro Foods
CAPONS
  Stock Yards Packing Co., Inc.
CAPONS, smoked
  McArthur's Smokehouse, Inc.
CAPPELLETTI
  Manganaro Foods
CAPRES
  Les Echalottes

CAPISCUM
  Magic Garden Herb Co.
  Rocky Hollow Herb Farm
CARAMEL nut swirl
  The Swiss Colony
CARAMEL pecan wheel
  The Swiss Colony
CARAMELS
  Manganaro Foods
CARAWAY
  Lhasa Karnak Herb Co.
  Magic Garden Herb Co.
  Paprikas Weiss Importer
  Sahadi Import Co.
CARAWAY beef
  The Swiss Colony
CARAWAY flavoring
  Paprikas Weiss Importer
CARAWAY, Russian black
  Roth and Son
CARAWAY seeds (brown and
    black)
  Aphrodesia
  Rocky Hollow Herb Farm
  Roth and Sons
CARDAMON
  Aphrodesia
  Lhasa Karnak Herb Co.
  Magic Garden Herb Co.
  Paprikas Weiss Importer
  Roth and Son
CARDAMON, Lebanese green
  Sahadi Import Co.
CARDAMON seeds, black
  Sahadi Import Co.
CARDAMON seeds, green
  Rocky Hollow Herb Farm

CAROB products
Deer Valley Farm
Jaffe Bros. Natural Foods
L. & L. Health Foods Co.
Old Town Natural Foods
Paprikas Weiss Importer
Rocky Hollow Herb Farm
Roth and Son
Sahadi Import Co.
CARROT seeds, wild
Rocky Hollow Herb Farm
CARROTS
Charlotte Charles, Inc.
Deer Valley Farm
Les Echalottes
CARROTS, baby
Paprikas Weiss Importer
CARROTS, miniature
Manganaro Foods
CASCADE red
Manganaro Foods
CASCARA bark
Magic Garden Herb Co.
CASHEWS
Jaffe Bros. Natural Foods
Kakawateez, Limited
Paprikas Weiss Importer
Rocky Hollow Herb Farm
Sahadi Import Co.
The Swiss Colony
CASSIA bark
Aphrodesia
CASSIS (black currant)
Les Echalottes
CASSIS, creme
Manganaro Foods
CATNIP
Aphrodesia

Old Town Natural Foods
Rocky Hollow Herb Farm
Roth and Son
CATNIP, leaves and tops, cut
Roth and Sons
CAULIFLOWER/cauliflower
products
Charlotte Charles, Inc.
Victoria Packing Corp.
CAVIAR
Bissinger's
Manganaro Foods
CAVIAR, Beluga
Charlotte Charles, Inc.
Omaha Steaks International
CAVIAR, black
Manganaro Foods
CAVIAR, lumpfish
Charlotte Charles, Inc.
Manganaro Foods
CAVIAR, salmon
Charlotte Charles, Inc.
Les Echalottes
CAVIAR, sturgeon
Les Echalottes
CAYENNE
Aphrodesia
Deer Valley Farm
The Herb Lady
Lhasa Karnak Herb Co.
Roth and Son
CEDAR powder
Aphrodesia
CELANDINE herb
Magic Garden Herb Co.
CELERY
Charlotte Charles, Inc.
Paprikas Weiss Importer

CELERY flakes
Aphrodesia
CELERY knobs, sliced
Les Echalottes
CELERY salt
Roth and Son
CELERY seasoning
Paprikas Weiss Importer
CELERY seed
Aphrodesia
Paprikas Weiss Importer
Rocky Hollow Herb Farm
Roth and Son
CENTAURY herb
Aphrodesia
Lhasa Karnak Herb Co.
Paprikas Weiss Importer
Rocky Hollow Herb Farm
CEPES
Les Echalottes
CEREALS, barley
Deer Valley Farm
CEREALS, cracked wheat
Paprikas Weiss Importer
CEREALS, dry
Charlotte Charles, Inc.
CEREALS, Famillia
Paprikas Weiss Importer
CEREALS, farina
Paprikas Weiss Importer
Roth and Son
CEREALS, granola
Rocky Hollow Herb Farm
CEREALS, mixed
The Appleyard Corporation
Deer Valley Farm
CEREALS, ready to serve
Deer Valley Farm

CEREALS, rice
Chico-San, Inc.
CERVELAT
Amana Society
Schaller and Weber, Inc.
CHAMOMILE (see also Camomille)
Aphrodesia
The Herb Lady
Lhasa Karnak Herb Co.
Magic Garden Herb Co.
Paprikas Weiss Importer
Rocky Hollow Herb Farm
Roth and Son
Sahadi Import Co.
CHAMPAGNE biscuits
Les Echalottes
CHANTERELLES
Les Echalottes
CHAPPARAL
Aphrodesia
Lhasa Karnak Herb Co.
Old Town Natural Foods
Rocky Hollow Herb Farm
CHARCOAL seasoning salt
Paprikas Weiss Importer
CHATEAUBRIAND
Omaha Steaks International
CHEDDI-beef
The Swiss Colony
CHEESE (see also under specific
type, e.g. Pecan-cheese ball,
etc.)
CHEESE, American
The Swiss Colony
CHEESE and meat
The Swiss Colony
CHEESE and salami
The Swiss Colony

CHEESE, Asiago
  Manganaro Foods
CHEESE, Austrian
  Cheese of All Nations
CHEESE, baby gouda
  Manganaro Foods
CHEESE, blue
  Cheese of All Nations
  Manganaro Foods
  Sugarbush Farm, Inc.
  Swiss Cheese Shops, Inc.
  The Swiss Colony
CHEESE, braided
  Sahadi Import Co.
CHEESE, brick
  The Swiss Colony
CHEESE, Bon Bel
  Manganaro Foods
CHEESE, brie
  Cheese of All Nations
CHEESE, bryndza
  Paprikas Weiss Importer
CHEESE, cacciocavallo
  Manganaro Foods
CHEESE, camembert
  Cheese of All Nations
  Manganaro Foods
CHEESE, caraway
  The Swiss Colony
CHEESE, cheddar
  Amana Society
  Cheese of All Nations
  Dakin Farm
  Deer Valley Farm
  Manganaro Foods
  Sugarbush Farm, Inc.
  Swiss Cheese Shops, Inc.
  The Swiss Colony

CHEESE, cheddar—Canadian
  Manganaro Foods
CHEESE, cheddar club
  The Swiss Colony
CHEESE, cheddar, sharp
  The Swiss Colony
CHEESE, cheddar with almond logs
  The Swiss Colony
CHEESE, cheddar with bacon
  The Swiss Colony
CHEESE, cheddar with onion
  The Swiss Colony
CHEESE, cheddar with pecan
  The Swiss Colony
CHEESE, cheddar with port wine
  The Swiss Colony
CHEESE, cheddar with sherry
  The Swiss Colony
CHEESE, cheddar with walnuts
  The Swiss Colony
CHEESE, colby
  Cheese of All Nations
  Swiss Cheese Shops, Inc.
  The Swiss Colony
CHEESE, coon
  Cheese of All Nations
CHEESE, cream
  Cheese of All Nations
CHEESE, edam
  Cheese of All Nations
  Manganaro Foods
  The Swiss Colony
CHEESE, emmentaler
  Manganaro Foods
CHEESE, England
  Cheese of All Nations

CHEESE, Finland
  Cheese of All Nations
CHEESE, fiore sardo
  Manganaro Foods
CHEESE, fonduta
  Manganaro Foods
CHEESE, fontina
  Manganaro Foods
CHEESE, France
  Breman House, Inc.
  Cheese of All Nations
CHEESE, French fontina
  Manganaro Foods
CHEESE, French gruyere
  Manganaro Foods
CHEESE, fruilana
  Manganaro Foods
CHEESE, Germany
  Breman House, Inc.
  Cheese of All Nations
CHEESE, goats' milk
  Cheese of All Nations
  Diamond Dairy Goat Farm
CHEESE, gorgonzola
  Manganaro Foods
CHEESE, gouda
  Cheese of All Nations
  The Swiss Colony
CHEESE, gouda, smoked
  The Swiss Colony
CHEESE, gouda with caraway
  The Swiss Colony
CHEESE, Greek
  Sahadi Import Co.
CHEESE, gruyere
  Cheese of All Nations

The Swiss Colony
CHEESE, halloum
  Sahadi Import Co.
CHEESE, hickory smoked
  Cheese of All Nations
  Dakin Farm
  Sugarbush Farm, Inc.
  The Swiss Colony
CHEESE, incannestrata
  Manganaro Foods
CHEESE, Ireland
  Cheese of All Nations
CHEESE, Israel
  Cheese of All Nations
CHEESE, Italy
  Cheese of All Nations
CHEESE, kashkawan
  Sahadi Import Co.
CHEESE, kefolitiri
  Sahadi Import Co.
CHEESE, limburger
  Cheese of All Nations
  Swiss Cheese Shops, Inc.
CHEESE, lion
  Manganaro Foods
CHEESE, longhorn
  Cheese of All Nations
CHEESE, long horn cheddar
  The Swiss Colony
CHEESE, low fat
  Cheese of All Nations
CHEESE, Mexico
  Cheese of All Nations
CHEESE, mizitri
  Sahadi Import Co.

CHEESE, Monterey jack
  Cheese of All Nations
CHEESE, mozzarella
  Cheese of All Nations
  Manganaro Foods
CHEESE, muenster
  Cheese of All Nations
  Swiss Cheese Shops, Inc.
  The Swiss Colony
CHEESE, Norway
  Cheese of All Nations
CHEESE, paprika
  The Swiss Colony
CHEESE, parenyica
  Paprikas Weiss Importer
CHEESE, parmesan
  Cheese of All Nations
CHEESE, parmicjiano
  Manganaro Foods
CHEESE, pecorino romano
  Manganaro Foods
CHEESE, pecorino di Tavola
  Manganaro Foods
CHEESE, Pennsylvania Dutch
  Cheese of All Nations
CHEESE, pepper
  The Swiss Colony
CHEESE, Poland
  Cheese of All Nations
CHEESE, portsalut
  Cheese of All Nations
  Manganaro Foods
  The Swiss Colony
CHEESE, Portugal
  Cheese of All Nations

CHEESE products
  Amana Society
CHEESE, provoletti
  Manganaro Foods
CHEESE, provolone
  Cheese of All Nations
  Manganaro Foods
CHEESE, ragusano
  Manganaro Foods
CHEESE, redcoat cheddar
  The Swiss Colony
CHEESE, ricotta
  Manganaro Foods
CHEESE, ricotta romano
  Manganaro Foods
CHEESE, ricotta siciliano
  Manganaro Foods
CHEESE, romanello
  Cheese of All Nations
CHEESE, romano
  Cheese of All Nations
CHEESE, roquefort
  Manganaro Foods
CHEESE, Roumania
  Cheese of All Nations
CHEESE, samsoe
  The Swiss Colony
CHEESE, sheeps' milk
  Cheese of All Nations
CHEESE souffle
  Les Echalottes
CHEESE, Spain
  Cheese of All Nations
CHEESE, stilton
  Cheese of All Nations
CHEESE, Sweden
  Cheese of All Nations

CHEESE, Swiss
  Cheese of All Nations
  Deer Valley Farm
  Manganaro Foods
  Swiss Cheese Shops, Inc.
  The Swiss Colony
CHEESE, Swiss fontina
  Manganaro Foods
CHEESE, Switzerland
  Breman House, Inc.
  Cheese of All Nations
CHEESE, Syrian
  Sahadi Import Co.
CHEESE, taleggio
  Manganaro Foods
CHEESE, tao-foo
  Cheese of All Nations
CHEESE, tybo
  Cheese of All Nations
CHEESE, Vermont
  The Appleyard Corporation
  Cheese of All Nations
  Crowley Cheese, Inc.
  Embassy Seafoods
  Sugarbush Farm, Inc.
CHEESE, Wisconsin
  Cheese of All Nations
  Deer Valley Farm
  Swiss Cheese Shops, Inc.
CHERRIES
  The Swiss Colony
CHERRIES, bing, dried
  Rocky Hollow Herb Farm
CHERRIES, candied, green
  Paprikas Weiss Importer
CHERRIES, candied, red
  Paprikas Weiss Importer

CHERRIES, dried
  Aphrodesia
  Roth and Son
CHERRIES in brandy
  Manganaro Foods
  Les Echalottes
CHERRIES in cherry liquer
  Paprikas Weiss Importer
CHERRIES in syrup, sour
  Paprikas Weiss Importer
CHERRIES, maraschino
  Charlotte Charles, Inc.
  Victoria Packing Corp.
CHERRIES, red
  Deer Valley Farm
CHERRIES, wild, pitted
  Manganaro Foods
CHERRY brandy snow cake roll
  The Swiss Colony
CHERRY cordial cake
  The Swiss Colony
CHERRY elderberry preserves
  The Swiss Colony
CHERRY flavoring
  Paprikas Weiss Importer
CHERRY jam
  Sahadi Import Co.
CHERRY seeds
  Aphrodesia
CHERRY stems
  Aphrodesia
  Roth and Son
CHERVIL
  Aphrodesia
  Deer Valley Farm
  Lhasa Karnak Herb Co.
  Paprikas Weiss Importer
  Rocky Hollow Herb Farm
  Roth and Son

CHESTNUT flour
  Manganaro Foods
  Paprikas Weiss Importer
  Roth and Son
CHESTNUT puree
  Paprikas Weiss Importer
CHESTNUT stuffing
  Les Echalottes
  Paprikas Weiss Importer
CHESTNUTS (see also Marrons)
  Rocky Hollow Herb Farm
  Roth and Son
CHESTNUTS, baby, in cognac
  Paprikas Weiss Importer
CHESTNUTS, dried
  Manganaro Foods
  Paprikas Weiss Importer
CHESTNUTS, whole, in brine
  Les Echalottes
  Paprikas Weiss Importer
CHICK pea flour
  Manganaro Foods
  Sahadi Import Co.
  Roth and Son
CHICK peas
  Les Echalottes
  Paprikas Weiss Importer
  Rocky Hollow Herb Farm
  Sahadi Import Co.
CHICK peas, roasted
  Sahadi Import Co.
CHICK peas, salted
  Sahadi Import Co.
CHICK peas, sugar coated
  Sahadi Import Co.
CHICKEN a la Kiev
  Stock Yards Packing Co., Inc.
  The Swiss Colony

CHICKEN a la Regal
  The Swiss Colony
CHICKEN consomme
  Paprikas Weiss Importer
CHICKEN cordon bleu
  Omaha Steaks International
  The Swiss Colony
CHICKEN cubes
  Paprikas Weiss Importer
CHICKEN, fried, seasoning
  Paprikas Weiss Importer
CHICKENS, smoked
  Ozark Mountain Smoke House,
    Inc.
CHICKWEED
  Aphrodesia
  Magic Garden Herb Co.
  Old Town Natural Foods
CHICORY
  Empire Coffee and Tea Co.
  Lhasa Karnak Herb Co.
CHICORY root, roasted
  Old Town Natural Foods
  Rocky Hollow Herb Farm
CHIDORI senbei
  Katagiri
CHILI bean dip
  Les Echalottes
CHILI con carne
  Charlotte Charles, Inc.
  Deer Valley Farm
  Smithfield Ham and Products
    Co., Inc.
CHILI con queso
  Les Echalottes
CHILI, green, peeled
  Les Echalottes

CHILI paste
  Kam Shing Co.
  Les Echalottes
CHILI peppers
  Aphrodesia
  Paprikas Weiss Importer
  Rocky Hollow Herb Farm
  Roth and Son
  Sahadi Import Co.
CHILI powder
  Aphrodesia
  Paprikas Weiss Importer
  Roth and Son
CHILIES, whole
  Kalustyan
  Paprikas Weiss, Importer
CHILLY pickle
  Sahadi Import Co.
CHIPS, corn
  Chico-San, Inc.
CHIPS, rice
  Chico-San, Inc.
CHIRETTA herb
  Magic Garden Herb Co.
CHIRIMENZAKO (Iriko)
  Katagiri
CHIVES
  Aphrodesia
  Paprikas Weiss Importer
  Rocky Hollow Herb Farm
CHOCOLATE almonds
  Paprikas Weiss Importer
CHOCOLATE, baking (see Baking
  chocolate)
CHOCOLATE balls
  The Swiss Colony
CHOCOLATE Christmas cake
  The Swiss Colony

CHOCOLATE creme wafers
  The Swiss Colony
CHOCOLATE, filled
  Bailey's of Boston, Inc.
  Bissinger's
  Catherine's Chocolate Shop
  Paprikas Weiss Importer
CHOCOLATE house
  The Swiss Colony
CHOCOLATE, milk
  Bissinger's
  Paprikas Weiss Importer
CHOCOLATE mints
  The Swiss Colony
CHOCOLATE mocha beans
  Paprikas Weiss Importer
CHOCOLATE oranges
  Paprikas Weiss Importer
CHOCOLATE pecan logs
  The Swiss Colony
CHOCOLATE, Swiss
  Charlotte Charles, Inc.
  Paprikas Weiss Importer
CHOCOLATE yule wreath
  The Swiss Colony
CHOCOLATES, summer coating,
    brown, green, pink, white
  Roth and Son
CHOCOLATES, "Szerencs"
  Paprikas Weiss Importer
CHOPPED liver (see Pates)
CHOW chow
  Deer Valley Farm
CHOWDERS/bisques
  Charlotte Charles, Inc.
  Clambake International, Inc.
CHRISTMAS butter
  The Swiss Colony

CHRISTMAS chocolates, slipper
    bon bons, Santa Claus
    Roth and Son
CHRISTMAS cremes
    Paprikas Weiss Importer
CHRISTMAS mints
    The Swiss Colony
CHRISTMAS mix candy
    The Swiss Colony
CHRYSANTHEMUM crystals
    Paprikas Weiss Importer
CHRYSANTHEMUM flowers
    Aphrodesia
CHUKASOBA
    Katagiri
CHUTNEY
    The Appleyard Corporation
    Kalustyan
    Les Echalottes
CHUTNEY, hot mango
    Les Echalottes
CHUTNEY, Indian, Colonel Skinner
    Les Echalottes
CHUTNEY, Indian, Major Grey
    Les Echalottes
CHUTNEY pickle
    Sahadi Import Co.
CILANTRO seed
    Old Town Natural Foods
CINCHONA bark
    Magic Garden Herb Co.
CINNAMON
    Aphrodesia
    Deer Valley Farm
    Lhasa Karnak Herb Co.
    Paprikas Weiss Importer
    Rocky Hollow Herb Farm

Roth and Son
Sahadi Import Co.
Victoria Packing Co.
CINNAMON apple pancake mix
    The Swiss Colony
CINNAMON apple preserves
    The Swiss Colony
CINNAMON hearts (red hots)
    Roth and Son
CIPOLLINI
    Victoria Packing Corp.
CITRIC acid
    Sahadi Import Co.
CITRON, candied
    Paprikas Weiss Importer
    Roth and Son
CLAM sauce, red
    Manganaro Foods
CLAMS, baby
    Manganaro Foods
CLAMS, baby, boiled
    Les Echalottes
CLAMS/clam products
    Charlotte Charles, Inc.
    Clambake International,
    Embassy Seafoods
    Sahadi Import Co.
    Saltwater Farm
CLAMS, smoked
    Les Echalottes
CLARIFIED butter (see Butter,
    clarified)
CLOS du Verdet
    Manganaro Foods
CLOVER blossoms, red
    Aphrodesia
    Old Town Natural Foods

Rocky Hollow Herb Farm
Roth and Sons
CLOVES
Aphrodesia
Empire Coffee and Tea
Company
Lhasa Karnak Herb Co.
Magic Garden Herb Co.
Paprikas Weiss Importer
Rocky Hollow Herb Farm
Roth and Son
Sahadi Import Co.
Victoria Packing Corp.
COCKTAIL frankfurters, Danish
Les Echalottes
COCKTAIL mixes
Bissinger's
COCKTAIL snacks, cheese
Byrd Cookie Co.
Deer Valley Farm
COCKTAIL snacks, corn
Charlotte Charles, Inc.
COCKTAIL snacks, onion/garlic
Byrd Cookie Co.
COCOA
Breman House, Inc.
Charlotte Charles, Inc.
Roth and Sons
COCOA almonds
Paprikas Weiss Importer
COCOA flavoring
Paprikas Weiss Importer
COCONUT
Kalustyan
COCONUT, cream of
Kam Shing Co.
COCONUT flavoring
Paprikas Weiss Importer

COCONUT oil
Sahadi Import Co.
COCONUT patties
The Swiss Colony
COCONUT syrup
Les Echalottes
COCONUTS/coconut products
Charlotte Charles, Inc.
Deer Valley Farm
Kalustyan
COCONUTS, shredded
Paprikas Weiss Importer
COFFEE, anisette
Manganaro Foods
COFFEE beans
Plumridge
COFFEE, blends
Caravel Coffee Co.
Empire Coffee and Tea Co.
Northwestern Coffee Mills
Schapira Coffee Co.
COFFEE, Brazil
Empire Coffee and Tea Co.
Northwestern Coffee Mills
Paprikas Weiss Importer
COFFEE, Columbia
Empire Coffee and Tea Co.
Northwestern Coffee Mills
COFFEE, Costa Rica
Empire Coffee and Tea Co.
COFFEE, decaffeinated
Breman House, Inc.
Empire Coffee and Tea Co.
Northwestern Coffee Mills
Schapira Coffee Co.
COFFEE, demitasse, instant
Manganaro Foods

COFFEE, espresso, Motta
Les Echalottes
COFFEE, Franck's chicory
PAP
Paprikas Weiss Importer
COFFEE, French roast
Empire Coffee and Tea Co.
Northwestern Coffee Mills
Paprikas Weiss Importer
COFFEE, German, decaffeinated
Paprikas Weiss Importer
COFFEE, Guatemala
Schapira Coffee Co.
COFFEE, Guatemalan Antigua
Paprikas Weiss Importer
COFFEE, Hawaiian
Charlotte Charles, Inc.
Empire Coffee and Tea Co.
COFFEE, Hungarian blend
Paprikas Weiss Importer
COFFEE, imported
Breman House, Inc.
COFFEE, instant
Empire Coffee and Tea Co.
Northwestern Coffee Mills
COFFEE, Italian espresso
Paprikas Weiss Importer
COFFEE, Italian roast
Empire Coffee and Tea Co.
COFFEE, Jamaica blue mountain
Paprikas Weiss Importer
COFFEE, Jamaican
Empire Coffee and Tea Co.
COFFEE, Java
Empire Coffee and Tea Co
Northwestern Coffee Mills
Schapira Coffee Co.
COFFEE, Kenya
Empire Coffee and Tea Co.

COFFEE, Kona
Paprikas Weiss Importer
COFFEE, malt
Paprikas Weiss Importer
COFFEE, Medaglia d'Oro
Manganaro Foods
COFFEE, Medaglia d'Oro espresso
Les Echalottes
COFFEE, medellin
Paprikas Weiss Importer
COFFEE, Mexico
Empire Coffee and Tea Co.
Schapira Coffee Co.
COFFEE, mid-east style dark
Sahadi Import Co.
COFFEE, mocha
Empire Coffee and Tea Co.
Northwestern Coffee Mills
COFFEE, mocha-java
Paprikas Weiss Importer
COFFEE, Motta and Perugina
Manganaro Foods
COFFEE, Motta espresso
Manganaro Foods
COFFEE royals
Roth and Son
COFFEE, Tanzania
Empire Coffee and Tea Co.
Paprikas Weiss Importer
COFFEE, Turkey
Empire Coffee and Tea Co.
COFFEE, Turkish
Paprikas Weiss Importer
COFFEE, unroasted
Empire Coffee and Tea Co.
Paprikas Weiss Importer
COFFEE, Venezuela
Empire Coffee and Tea Co.
Schapira Coffee Co.

COFFEE, Viennese roast
Paprikas Weiss Importer
COFFEE, Vivo
Manganaro Foods
COHOSH, black
Aphrodesia
Magic Garden Herb Co.
Old Town Natural Foods
Rocky Hollow Herb Farm
COHOSH, blue
Aphrodesia
Magic Garden Herb Co.
Old Town Natural Foods
COLA nuts
Aphrodesia
Lhasa Karnak Herb Co.
COLOMBA
Manganaro Foods
COLTSFOOT
Aphrodesia
Lhasa Karnak Herb Co.
Old Town Natural Foods
Rocky Hollow Herb Farm
COLUMBO root
Magic Garden Herb Co.
COMFREY
Aphrodesia
The Herb Lady
Lhasa Karnak Herb Co.
Lone Organic Farm
Magic Garden Herb Co.
Old Town Natural Foods
COMFREY root
Rocky Hollow Herb Farm
CONFECTIONS, European
Breman House, Inc.
CONFETTI
Manganaro Foods

COOKIES, butter
Deer Valley Farm
The Swiss Colony
COOKIES, chocolate chip
Charlotte Charles, Inc.
COOKIES, cream filled
Byrd Cookie Co.
COOKIES, fortune
Charlotte Charles, Inc.
Oriental Country Store
COOKIES, ginger
Charlotte Charles, Inc.
COOKIES, imported
Breman House, Inc.
COOKIES, lemon
Charlotte Charles, Inc.
COOKIES, molasses
Deer Valley Farm
COOKIES, oatmeal
Deer Valley Farm
COOKIES, old world
The Swiss Colony
COOKIES, orange
Charlotte Charles, Inc.
COOKIES, peanut butter
Deer Valley Farm
COOKIES, vanilla
Charlotte Charles, Inc.
COPPA
Manganaro Foods
COQUILLETTES
Les Echalottes
CORDIAL cakes
The Swiss Colony
CORIANDER
Aphrodesia
Deer Valley Farm
Lhasa Karnak Herb Co.

Paprikas Weiss Importer
Roth and Son
CORIANDER seeds
Magic Garden Herb Co.
Rocky Hollow Herb Farm
Sahadi Import Co.
CORIANDER, sugar coated
Sahadi Import Co.
CORN
Charlotte Charles, Inc.
Deer Valley Farm
CORN chips (see Chips, corn)
CORN, crushed
Paprikas Weiss Importer
CORN flowers
Aphrodesia
CORN meal
Paprikas Weiss Importer
Roth and Son
CORN starch
Paprikas Weiss Importer
Roth and Son
CORNED beef
McArthur's Smokehouse, Inc.
Omaha Steaks International
CORNED beef and cabbage
Paprikas Weiss Importer
CORNISH game hens
Omaha Steaks International
Stock Yards Packing Co., Inc.
The Swiss Colony
CORN on cob seasoning
Paprikas Weiss Importer
COTECHINI
Manganaro Foods
COUS-cous
Les Echalottes
Rocky Hollow Herb Farm
Sahadi Import Co.

CRABAPPLES
Charlotte Charles, Inc.
CRABMEAT, king
Les Echalottes
CRABS, bisque
Les Echalottes
CRABS/crab products
R. H. Chamberlin
Charlotte Charles, Inc.
Embassy Seafoods
Omaha Steaks International
Saltwater Farm
CRACKERS/wafers, cheese
Deer Valley Farm
CRACKERS/wafers, European
Breman House, Inc.
CRACKERS/wafers, graham
Deer Valley Farm
CRACKERS/wafers, oriental
Bissinger's
Charlotte Charles, Inc.
CRACKERS/wafers, seed
Byrd Cookie Co.
Charlotte Charles, Inc.
CRACKERS/wafers, whole wheat
Deer Valley Farm
CRAMP bark
Magic Garden Herb Co.
CRANBERRY sauce
Deer Valley Farm
CRANESBILL root
Rocky Hollow Herb Farm
CRAWFISH, bisque
Rocky Hollow Herb Farm
CRAWFISH, bisque
Les Echalottes
CREAM of tartar
Paprikas Weiss Importer
Roth and Son

CREAM stabilizer
  Roth and Son
CREME de cocoa cordial cake
  The Swiss Colony
CREME de cocoa yule log
  The Swiss Colony
CREME de marrons
  Les Echalottes
CREME de menthe flavoring
  Paprikas Weiss Importer
CREME de menthe torte
  The Swiss Colony
CREOLE seasoning
  Paprikas Weiss Importer
CREPE suzette
  Les Echalottes
CREPES/crepe mixes
  Charlotte Charles, Inc.
CRYSTALLIZED anise seed
  Roth and Son
CRYSTALLIZED assorted flowers
  Les Echalottes
CRYSTALLIZED decorator flowers
  Paprikas Weiss Importer
CRYSTALLIZED Canton ginger
  Paprikas Weiss Importer
CRYSTALLIZED coriander seed
  Roth and Son
CRYSTALLIZED cumin seed
  Roth and Son
CRYSTALLIZED ginger, sliced
  Les Echalottes
CRYSTALLIZED lavender
  Roth and Son
CRYSTALLIZED lilacs
  Les Echalottes
  Roth and Son
CRYSTALIZED mimosa
  Roth and Son

CRYSTALLIZED mint leaves
  Les Echalottes
  Roth and Son
CRYSTALLIZED rose petals
  Les Echalottes
  Roth and Son
CRYSTALLIZED roses, whole
  Les Echalottes
  Roth and Son
CRYSTALLIZED sugar
  Paprikas Weiss Importer
  Roth and Son
CRYSTALLIZED violets
  Les Echalottes
  Roth and Son
CUBEB berries
  Aphrodesia
CUCUMBER, pickled
  Kam Shing Co.
CUMIN seed
  Aphrodesia
  Magic Garden Herb Co.
  Paprikas Weiss Importer
  Rocky Hollow Herb Farm
  Roth and Son
  Sahadi Import Co.
CURRANTS (see also Black
    currants)
  Old Town Natural Foods
CURRANTS, dried
  Rocky Hollow Herb Farm
CURRANTS, dried and candied
  Roth and Son
CURRIED beef pie with gravy
  Les Echalottes
CURRY
  Deer Valley Farm
  Paprikas Weiss Importer
  Rocky Hollow Herb Farm

CURRY, Indian
 Katagiri
CURRY paste
 Les Echalottes
CURRY powder
 Aphrodesia
 Katagiri
 Les Echalottes
 Roth and Son
 Sahadi Import Co.
CURRY, risotto
 Manganaro Foods
CURRY sauce
 Les Echalottes
CURRY sauce mix
 Paprikas Weiss Importer
CURRY, Vermont house
 Katagiri
CUTTLEFISH, seasoned
 Kam Shing Co.
DAIKAKU okaki
 Katagiri
DAISY flowers
 Aphrodesia
DAIZU
 Katagiri
DAKKA (mixed spices)
 Sahadi Import Co.
DALLS
 Kalustyan
DAMIANA
 Aphrodesia
 The Herb Lady
 Lhasa Karnak Herb Co.
 Magic Garden Herb Co.
 Old Town Natural Foods
 Rocky Hollow Herb Farm

DANDELION
 Aphrodesia
 Old Town Natural Foods
DANDELION leaves
 Rocky Hollow Herb Farm
 Roth and Son
DANDELION root
 Roth and Son
DANISH pastries
 Deer Valley Farm
DASHIKOBU
 Katagiri
DASHI-no-moto
 Katagiri
DASHIZAKO (Iriko)
 Katagiri
DATE jam
 Sahadi Import Co.
DATES
 Jaffe Bros. Natural Foods
 L. &. L. Health Foods Co.
 Sahadi Import Co.
 The Swiss Colony
DATES, California
 Sahadi Import Co.
DATES, dried and candied
 Roth and Son
DATES, pecan stuffed
 Priester's Pecans
DATES, preserved
 Paprikas Weiss Importer
DEER (see Venison)
DEER'S tongue
 Aphrodesia
DESSERT toppings
 Bailey's of Boston, Inc.
 Charlotte Charles, Inc.

DIETETIC products
  Catherine's Chocolate Shop
  Estee Candy Co., Inc.
DILL
  Aphrodesia
  Lhasa Karnak Herb Co.
DILL, cut
  Roth and Son
DILL, dried
  Roth and Son
DILL seed
  Magic Garden Herb Co.
  Rocky Hollow Herb Farm
DILL weed
  Rocky Hollow Herb Farm
DIPS/spreads, Mexican
  Charlotte Charles, Inc.
DITTANY of Crete
  Aphrodesia
  Rocky Hollow Herb Farm
DOBOSH, almond
  The Swiss Colony
DOBOSH, butter creme
  The Swiss Colony
DOBOSH, creme de menthe
  The Swiss Colony
DOBOSH, double chocolate
  The Swiss Colony
DOBOSH, fudge nut
  The Swiss Colony
DOBOSH torte
  Paprikas Weiss Importer
  The Swiss Colony
DONG quai (Korean)
  Aphrodesia
DOUGH for baklawa
  Sahadi Import Co.
DOUGH for burma
  Sahadi Import Co.

DRAGON'S blood powder
  Aphrodesia
DUCK a l'orange
  Omaha Steaks International
DUCK, Bombay
  Kalustyan
  Les Echalottes
DUCK egg, salted
  Kam Shing Co.
DULSE
  Magic Garden Herb Co.
DUMPLING mix, potato
  Paprikas Weiss Importer
DUMPLINGS/dumpling mixes
  Charlotte Charles, Inc.
DUTCH gaufrettes
  Les Echalottes
DUTCH gaufrettes wafers
  Paprikas Weiss Importer
ECHINACEA
  Aphrodesia
EDAM triangles
  The Swiss Colony
EEL, jellied
  Les Echalottes
EEL, pickled
  Les Echalottes
EEL, smoked
  Les Echalottes
EGG barley pasta
  Paprikas Weiss Importer
EGG color
  Paprikas Weiss Importer
EGG noodle squares
  Paprikas Weiss Importer
EGG roll
  Kam Shing Co.
EGG, thousand year
  Oriental Country Store

EGGPLANT
  Victoria Packing Corp.
EGGPLANT, dried
  Sahadi Import Co.
EGGPLANT, pickled
  Sahadi Import Co.
EGGPLANT, stuffed
  Sahadi Import Co.
EGGPLANT, Turkish
  Paprikas Weiss Importer
EGGS, duck
  Swanjord Hatchery
EGGS, goose
  Swanjord Hatchery
EGGS, peacock
  Roth and Son
EGGS, quail
  Les Echalottes
EGGS, sparrow
  Swanjord Hatchery
EUJONI
  Katagiri
ELDER bark
  Lhasa Karnak Herb Co.
ELDER flowers
  Aphrodesia
  Magic Garden Herb Co.
  Old Town Natural Foods
  Paprikas Weiss Importer
  ROCKY
  Rocky Hollow Herb Farm
  Roth and Son
ELDERBERRY jelly
  Paprikas Weiss Importer
ELECAMPNE
  Aphrodesia
ELECAMPNE root
  Rocky Hollow Herb Farm

"ELISEN" lebkuchen
  Roth and Son
ELM bark slabs
  Roth and Son
ENCHILADA sauce
  Les Echalottes
ENCHILADAS, cheese
  Les Echalottes
ENDIVES
  Les Echalottes
  Manganaro Foods
  Paprikas Weiss Importer
EPAZOTE
  Aphrodesia
ESCARGOTS (see also Snails)
  Les Echalottes
  Manganaro Foods
ESCOFFIER sauce
  Les Echalottes
EUCALYPTUS leaves
  Magic Garden Herb Co.
  Old Town Natural Foods
  Rocky Hollow Herb Farm
  Roth and Son
EUPHORBIA herb
  Aphrodesia
EVERLASTING
  Rocky Hollow Herb Farm
EYEBRIGHT
  Aphrodesia
  Lhasa Karnak Herb Co.
  Rocky Hollow Herb Farm
FALERNUM
  Les Echalottes
FAMILLIA (see Cereals)
FARINHA de Mandioca
  Roth and Son
FARINA (see Cereals)

FAVA beans
  Sahadi Import Co.
FENNEL
  Empire Coffee and Tea Co.
  Victoria Packing Corp.
FENNEL seeds
  Aphrodesia
  The Herb Lady
  Lhasa Karnak Herb Co.
  Magic Garden Herb Co.
  Paprikas Weiss Importer
  Rocky Hollow Herb Farm
  Roth and Son
  Sahadi Import Co.
FENNEL seed, sugar coated
  Sahadi Import Co.
FENUGREEK
  The Herb Lady
  Sahadi Import Co.
FENUGREEK, ground
  Roth and Son
FENUGREEK leaves
  Rocky Hollow Herb Farm
FENUGREEK seed
  Aphrodesia
  Lhasa Karnak Herb Co.
  Magic Garden Herb Co.
  Old Town Natural Foods
  Paprikas Weiss Importer
  Roth and Son
FERNET Branca
  Manganaro Foods
FERRARA
  Manganaro Foods
FERRO china bisleri
  Manganaro Foods
FIG jam
  Sahadi Import Co.

FIGS
  Charlotte Charles, Inc.
  L. & L. Health Foods Co.
  Manganaro Foods
  Rocky Hollow Herb Farm
  Sahadi Import Co.
  The Swiss Colony
FIGS, dried and candied
  Roth and Son
FIGS, glazed Australian
  Sahadi Import Co.
FIGS, imported natural
  Sahadi Import Co.
FIGS, Smyrna
  Paprikas Weiss Importer
FILBERT nuts
  Jaffe Bros. Natural Foods
  Kakawateez, Limited
  Paprikas Weiss Importer
  Sahadi Import Co.
  The Swiss Colony
FINNAN haddie
  Embassy Seafoods
FISH chowder
  Embassy Seafoods
  Les Echalottes
  Saltwater Farm
FISH, freshwater
  Breman House, Inc.
FISH jellies
  Sahadi Import Co.
FISH stomach, fried
  Kam Shing Co.
FIVE finger grass
  Aphrodesia
FIVE spice powder
  Kam Shing Co.
  Oriental Country Store

FLAGEOLET beans
  Les Echalottes
  Manganaro Foods
  Paprikas Weiss Importer
  Roth and Son
FLAVE
  Katagiri
FLAVORING (see also under
    specific type, e.g. Juniper
    flavoring, Orange flavoring,
    etc.)
FLAVORING essences
  Breman House, Inc.
  Chico-San, Inc.
  Deer Valley Farm
FLAVORING, sour cherry
  Paprikas Weiss Importer
FLAVORINGS/extracts, soft drink
  Bacchanalia
FLAX seeds
  Aphrodesia
  Paprikas Weiss Importer
  Rocky Hollow Herb Farm
  Roth and Son
FLEABANE
  Aphrodesia
FLOUR (see also under specific
    type, e.g., Strudel flour)
FLOUR, barley
  Deer Valley Farm
FLOUR, graham
  Deer Valley Farm
  Kalustyan
FLOUR, oat
  Deer Valley Farm
  L. & L. Health Foods Co.
FLOUR, potato
  Deer Valley Farm

Paprikas Weiss Importer
Roth and Son
FLOUR, pumpernickel
  Roth and Son
FLOUR, rice
  Chico-San, Inc.
  Deer Valley Farm
  Kalustyan
  L. & L. Health Foods Co.
  Paprikas Weiss Importer
  Sahadi Import Co.
  Roth and Son
FLOUR, rye
  Deer Valley Farm
  L. & L. Health Foods Co.
  Old Town Natural Foods
  Paprikas Weiss Importer
  Roth and Son
FLOUR, soy
  Jaffe Bros. Natural Foods
  Old Town Natural Foods
  Paprikas Weiss Importer
  Roth and Son
FLOUR, soya
  L. & L. Health Foods Co.
FLOUR, wheat
  Deer Valley Farm
  Kalustyan
  L. & L. Health Foods Co.
  Old Town Natural Foods
FLOUR, white
  Deer Valley Farm
FLOUR, whole wheat
  Paprikas Weiss Importer
  Sahadi Import Co.
  Roth and Son
FLOURS/mixes, European
  Breman House, Inc.

FONDUE (see Swiss fondue)
FOOD colors
    Roth and Son
FOOD supplements/vitamins
    Deer Valley Farm
    De Sousa's—The Healthians
    Lone Organic Farm
    Wachters' Organic Sea Products
      Corp.
FO ti teng
    Aphrodesia
    Rocky Hollow Herb Farm
FRANKFURTERS
    Schaller and Weber, Inc.
FRANKFURTERS, cocktail (see
    Cocktail frankfurters)
FRANKINCENSE
    Magic Garden Herb Co.
FRENCH choucroute
    Les Echalottes
FREND grielles
    Manganaro Foods
FRUIT (see under specific type,
    e.g., Lemon, Papaya, etc.)
FRUIT and nut bars
    Charlotte Charles, Inc.
FRUIT cake
    Bailey's of Boston, Inc.
    Butterfield Farms, Inc.
    Charlotte Charles, Inc.
    Koinonia Products
    Priester's Pecans
    The Swiss Colony
    Young Pecan Sales Corp.
FRUIT cake, butter-rum
    The Swiss Colony
FRUIT cake, Irish
    Paprikas Weiss Importer

FRUIT cake, old Irish whiskey
    Les Echalottes
FRUIT, dried
    Bacchanalia
    Deer Valley Farm
    Jaffe Bros. Natural Foods
    Old Town Natural Foods
    The Swiss Colony
    Timber Crest Farms
FRUIT in brandy
    Manganaro Foods
FRUIT, mixed, dried and candied
    Roth and Son
FRUIT, mixed, fresh
    Bissinger's
FRUIT, "moisturized"
    The Swiss Colony
FRUIT rolls
    Sahadi Import Co.
FRUIT soup mixes
    Paprikas Weiss Importer
FRUITS in Jamaican rum
    Les Echalottes
FRUITS in liquers
    Charlotte Charles, Inc.
FRUITS in syrup, Greek
    Charlotte Charles, Inc.
FRUITS, salad
    Charlotte Charles, Inc.
FUDGE
    Bailey's of Boston, Inc.
    Breakfast Creek Farm
    Deer Valley Farm
FUDGE nut ring
    The Swiss Colony
FUDGE nut torte
    The Swiss Colony
FUDGE, pecan
    Priester's Pecans

FUJIMOTO, white (U.S.)
   Katagiri
FUJIYA, milky
   Katagiri
FUNGUS, dried
   Kam Shing Co.
FUNYU (U.S.)
   Katagiri
FURIKAKENORI
   Katagiri
FU tze powder
   The Herb Lady
GALANGAL
   Aphrodesia
GAME hen, smoked
   McArthur's Smokehouse, Inc.
GAME hens (see Poultry/game—
   Rock Cornish hens)
GARBIT
   Sahadi Import Co.
GARLIC
   Aphrodesia
   Deer Valley Farm
   Lhasa Karnak Herb Co.
   Paprikas Weiss Importer
   Rocky Hollow Herb Farm
   Sahadi Import Co.
   Victoria Packing Corp.
GARLIC powder
   Empire Coffee and Tea Company
   Roth and Son
GAUFRETTES (see Dutch gau-
   frettes)
GEFILTE fish
   Les Echalottes
   Paprikas Weiss Importer
GELATIN
   Roth and Son

GELATIN, powdered
   Paprikas Weiss Importer
GELATIN sheets, white
   Paprikas Weiss Importer
GENMAICHA
   Katagiri
GENTIAN
   Aphrodesia
GENTIAN root
   Rocky Hollow Herb Farm
GERMANDER herb
   Magic Garden Herb Co.
GHERKINS
   Manganaro Foods
GHERKINS, imported
   Paprikas Weiss Importer
GHERKINS in vinegar
   Les Echalottes
GIANDUIOTTI
   Manganaro Foods
GUARDINIERA
   Victoria Packing Corp.
GINGER (see also Crystallized
   ginger)
   Aphrodesia
   Charlotte Charles, Inc.
   Lhasa Karnak Herb Co.
   Oriental Country Store
   Rocky Hollow Herb Farm
   Roth and Son
   Sahadi Import Co.
GINGER cookies (see Cookies,
   ginger)
GINGER, dried and candied
   Roth and Son
GINGER marmalade
   Paprikas Weiss Importer
   Roth and Son

GINGER, preserved stem
Les Echalottes
GINGER preserves
Les Echalottes
Paprikas Weiss Importer
GINGER root
Magic Garden Herb Co.
Roth and Son
GINGERBREAD
The Swiss Colony
GINGERBREAD hearts
Roth and Son
GINGERBREAD spice
Paprikas Weiss Importer
GINSENG/ginseng products
Aphrodesia
Breman House, Inc.
Celestial Seasonings
De Sousa's—The Healthians
The Fmali Co.
The Herb Lady
Lhasa Karnak Herb Co.
Magic Garden Herb Co.
Rocky Hollow Herb Farm
Wonder Natural Foods
GNOCCHI, instant
Manganaro Foods
GOLD thread
Rocky Hollow Herb Farm
GOLDENROD
Lhasa Karnak Herb Co.
Rocky Hollow Herb Farm
GOLDENSEAL
Aphrodesia
The Fmali Co.
The Herb Lady
Lhasa Karnak Herb Co.

GOLDENSEAL root
Magic Garden Herb Co.
Old Town Natural Foods
Rocky Hollow Herb Farm
GOMA shio
Katagiri
GOMA, shvio, kuro
Katagiri
GOOSE fat, rendered
Paprikas Weiss Importer
GOOSE liver, chopped (see Pates)
GOTU cola
Aphrodesia
The Herb Lady
Lhasa Karnak Herb Co.
Magic Garden Herb Co.
Old Town Natural Foods
Rocky Hollow Herb Farm
GOUDA cheese crispies
Paprikas Weiss Importer
GOULASH, deer
Paprikas Weiss Importer
GOULASH, pork
Paprikas Weiss Importer
GOULASH spice mix
Roth and Son
GOULASH, wild boar
PAPRIKAS
Paprikas Weiss Importer
GRAHAM flour (see Flour, graham)
GRAINS of paradise
Aphrodesia
GRAISSE d'Oie
Les Echalottes
GRAM, black African
Rocky Hollow Herb Farm

GRAM dall
  Sahadi Import Co.
GRANOLA (see Cereals)
GRAPE delight
  Sahadi Import Co.
GRAPE leaves
  Paprikas Weiss Importer
GRAPEFRUIT
  Bissinger's
  Lee's Fruit Co., Inc.
  The Swiss Colony
GRAPEFRUIT, fresh
  R. H. Chamberlin
  Deer Valley Farm
GRAPEFRUIT marmalade
  Les Echalottes
GRAPEFRUIT segments
  Charlotte Charles, Inc.
GREEK delight with almonds
  Sahadi Import Co.
GREEK specialties
  Charlotte Charles, Inc.
GRENADINE
  Les Echalottes
GROATS
  Deer Valley Farm
  Paprikas Weiss Importer
GUAIAC wood
  Magic Garden Herb Co.
GUARANA
  Aphrodesia
GUARAM masala
  Aphrodesia
GUAVA juice
  Sahadi Import Co.
GUAVA shells in syrup
  Sahadi Import Co.

GUIACUM chips
  Aphrodesia
GUM arabic
  Lhasa Karnak Herb Co.
  Rocky Hollow Herb Farm
GUM drops (see Candy, gum drops
GUMBO file
  Paprikas Weiss Importer
  Roth and Son
GYOKURO
  Katagiri
HABUCHA
  Katagiri
HACHIMITSU
  Katagiri
HAGENBUTTEN
  Roth and Son
HAJIKAMI
  Katagiri
HALAWA, chocolate
  Sahadi Import Co.
HALAWA, marble
  Sahadi Import Co.
HALAWA, plain
  Sahadi Import Co.
HALAWA, Turkish
  Sahadi Import Co.
HALAWA, vanilla
  Sahadi Import Co.
HALAWA with nuts
  Sahadi Import Co.
HALAWA with pistachio
  Sahadi Import Co.
HAM (see also Proscuitto)
  Stock Yards Packing Co., Inc.
  The Swiss Colony
HAM, Budapest
  Paprikas Weiss Importer

HAM, deviled
  Smithfield Ham and Products
    Co., Inc.
HAM, dry cured
  Omaha Steaks International
HAM, German smoked
  Paprikas Weiss Importer
HAM, Holland
  Charlotte Charles, Inc.
  The Swiss Colony
HAM roll
  The Swiss Colony
HAM, Smithfield
  V. W. Joyner and Company
  Smithfield Ham and Products
    Co., Inc.
HAM, smoked
  The Forsts
  McArthur's Smokehouse, Inc.
  Ozark Mountain Smoke House,
    Inc.
  Schaller and Weber, Inc.
HAMBURGER seasoning
  Paprikas Weiss Importer
HANAKATSUO
  Katagiri
HANARAKKYO
  Katagiri
HARE, fried
  Paprikas Weiss Importer
HARICOTS verts
  Paprikas Weiss Importer
HARIHARI-zuke
  Katagiri
HARISSA
  Les Echalottes
  Sahadi Import Co.
HARISSA, hot pepper spread
  Les Echalottes

HARUSAME/sai fun (China)
  Katagiri
HAW bark, black
  Aphrodesia
  Magic Garden Herb Co.
HAWAII sanbaizuke
  Katagiri
HAWAII takuwan
  Katagiri
HAWTHORNE berries
  Aphrodesia
  Rocky Hollow Herb Farm
  Roth and Son
HAYANIKOBU
  Katagiri
HAZELNUT crunch
  Roth and Son
HAZELNUTS
  Paprikas Weiss Importer
  Rocky Hollow Herb Farm
HEAL all
  Aphrodesia
HEARTS of palm
  Breman House, Inc.
  Les Echalottes
  Sahadi Import Co.
HELIOTROPIN
  Aphrodesia
HENNA
  Aphrodesia
  Rocky Hollow Herb Farm
  Sahadi Import Co.
HENNA leaves
  Magic Garden Herb Co.
HERBS (see under specific type,
    e.g. Eyebright, Goldenseal,
    etc.)

HERBS, aromatic
  Celestial Seasonings
  Deer Valley Farm
HERBS, blended
  Empire Coffee and Tea Company
HERRING/herring products
  Breman House, Inc.
  Charlotte Charles, Inc.
  Roth and Son
HERRING, kippered
  Les Echalottes
HIBISCUS flowers
  Aphrodesia
  Old Town Natural Foods
HICKORY bark
  Rocky Hollow Herb Farm
HICKORY smoke salt
  Paprikas Weiss Importer
HIGH John the conqueror root
  Aphrodesia
  Rocky Hollow Herb Farm
HIJIKI
  Katagiri
HI-me
  Katagiri
HIP fruit
  Paprikas Weiss Importer
  Roth and Son
HIRSCHONSALZ
  Paprikas Weiss Importer
  Roth and Son
HIYAMUGI
  Katagiri
HOLLANDAISE (see Sauce,
    Hollandaise)
HOLLYHOCK
  Rocky Hollow Herb Farm
HOMINY grits
  Roth and Son

HONEY, Bavarian pine
  Roth and Son
HONEY bread
  Paprikas Weiss Importer
  Roth and Son
HONEY cake
  Paprikas Weiss Importer
  Roth and Son
HONEY cake spice
  Roth and Son
HONEY, Central American coffee
    blossom
  Roth and Son
HONEY, clover
  Dakin Farm
  Thousand Island Apiaries
HONEY comb
  Roth and Son
HONEY, dark
  Sahadi Import Co.
HONEY, Dutch clover
  Roth and Son
HONEY, Dutch heather
  Roth and Son
HONEY filled drops
  Roth and Son
HONEY, French
  Manganaro Foods
HONEY, French lavender
  Roth and Son
HONEY, French rosemary
  Roth and Son
HONEY, German linden
  Roth and Son
HONEY, German pinewood
  Roth and Son
HONEY, Greek hymetius
  Roth and Son

141

HONEY, heather
  Paprikas Weiss Importer
HONEY, Hungarian
  Paprikas Weiss Importer
HONEY, Hungarian acacia
  Roth and Son
HONEY, imported
  Breman House, Inc.
  Deer Valley Farm
HONEY, Israeli kosher
  Roth and Son
HONEY, Italian
  Manganaro Foods
HONEY, linden
  Paprikas Weiss Importer
HONEY, orange blossom
  Charlotte Charles, Inc.
  Lee's Fruit Co., Inc.
  The Swiss Colony
HONEY, pine
  Paprikas Weiss Importer
HONEY, pure
  Sahadi Import Co.
HONEY, Spanish rosemary
  Roth and Son
HONEY, tupelo
  Deer Valley Farm
HONEY, wild flower
  Deer Valley Farm
HONEYSUCKLE flowers
  Aphrodesia
HOPS
  Aphrodesia
  Magic Garden Herb Co.
  Old Town Natural Foods
  Roth and Son
HOREHOUND candy (see Candy,
  horehound)

Aphrodesia
  Lhasa Karnak Herb Co.
  Paprikas Weiss Importer
  Rocky Hollow Herb Farm
  Roth and Son
HOREHOUND cough drops
  Roth and Son
HORSERADISH
  Deer Valley Farm
  Paprikas Weiss Importer
  Smithfield Ham and Products
    Co., Inc.
HORSETAIL
  Aphrodesia
  Magic Garden Herb Co.
HORSETAIL grass
  Rocky Hollow Herb Farm
HOSHIEBI
  Katagiri
HOSHI renkon (China)
  Katagiri
HOUMOUS-bi-tahini
  Sahadi Import Co.
HUCKLEBERRIES
  Aphrodesia
  Rocky Hollow Herb Farm
HYDROCOTYLE (fo-ti-tieng)
  Magic Garden Herb Co.
HYSSOP
  Aphrodesia
  Old Town Natural Foods
  Rocky Hollow Herb Farm
ICE cream powder
  Paprikas Weiss Importer
ICELAND moss
  Rocky Hollow Herb Farm
ICHIMI togarashi
  Katagiri

IKA shiokara
  Katagiri
IKARIMAME
  Katagiri
INDIAN nuts
  Sahadi Import Co.
INDIAN root, black
  Roth and Son
IRISH coffee flavored chocolate
    bar
  Roth and Son
IRISH moss
  Aphrodesia
  Lhasa Karnak Herb Co.
  Rocky Hollow Herb Farm
  Roth and Son
IRO ichiban
  Katagiri
ISAGO senbei
  Katagiri
ITALIAN herb blend
  Paprikas Weiss Importer
ITOKEZURI hanakatsuo
  Katagiri
ITAWAKAME
  Katagiri
IVY, ground
  Rocky Hollow Herb Farm
JABOURANDI leaves
  Aphrodesia
JAM, Hungarian
  Roth and Son
JAM, juniperberry
  Paprikas Weiss Importer
JAM, mastic
  Sahadi Import Co.
JAM of roses
  Manganaro Foods

JAM, plum
  Roth and Son
  Sahadi Import Co.
JAM, preiselbeeren
  Paprikas Weiss Importer
JAM, quince
  Paprikas Weiss Importer
  Sahadi Import Co.
JAM, raspberry
  Paprikas Weiss Importer
JAM, red cherry
  Paprikas Weiss Importer
JAM, red currant
  Paprikas Weiss Importer
JAM, rose petal
  Roth and Son
  Sahadi Import Co.
JAM, sour cherry
  Paprikas Weiss Importer
  Sahadi Import Co.
JAM, strawberry
  Old Town Natural Foods
  Paprikas Weiss Importer
  Sahadi Import Co.
JAM, Swiss plum
  Paprikas Weiss Importer
JAMS/jellies/preserves, fruit
  Charlotte Charles, Inc.
  Deer Valley Farm
  De Sousa's—The Healthians
JAMS/jellies/preserves, herb
  Deer Valley Farm
JAMS/jellies/preserves, wine
  Charlotte Charles, Inc.
JAPAN takuwan
  Katagiri
JELLY, apple cider
  The Appleyard Corporation

JELLY, quince
Les Echalottes
JELLY, raspberry
Sahadi Import Co.
JELLY, red currant
Les Echalottes
JELLY, rose petal
Les Echalottes
JERICHO (resurrection) flower
Aphrodesia
JERSEY tea root
Rocky Hollow Herb Farm
JEWELWEED
Aphrodesia
JINTAN
Katagiri
JOSHINKO
Katagiri
JUICE, apple
Charlotte Charles, Inc.
JUICE, apricot
Charlotte Charles, Inc.
JUICE, berry
Deer Valley Farm
Jaffe Bros. Natural Foods
JUICE, fruit
Deer Valley Farm
De Sousa's—The Healthians
Jaffe Bros. Natural Foods
JUICE, grapefruit
Charlotte Charles, Inc.
JUICE, mango
Sahadi Import Co.
JUICE, pineapple
Charlotte Charles, Inc.
JUICE, vegetable
Charlotte Charles, Inc.
Deer Valley Farm

JUNIPER berries
Aphrodesia
Lhasa Karnak Herb Co.
Magic Garden Herb Co.
Paprikas Weiss Importer
Rocky Hollow Herb Farm
Roth and Son
JUNIPER flavoring
Paprikas Weiss Importer
JUNSAI
Katagiri
KAHU foul mudammas
Sahadi Import Co.
KAKIMOCHI
Katagiri
KAKUKIRI kobu
Katagiri
KAMPYO
Katagiri
KANTEN (shiro or aka)
Katagiri
KAPPA tengoku (kywii)
Katagiri
KARASHI kobu
Katagiri
KASHA (see Groats)
KATAKURIKO
Katagiri
KATAYIF, almond filled
Sahadi Import Co.
KATSUO dashi-no-moto
Katagiri
KATSUO mirinyaki
Katagiri
KATSUO shiokara
Katagiri
KATSUODENBU
Katagiri

KAURAYANAGI bancha
Katagiri
KAVA-kava root
Magic Garden Herb Co.
KELP
Aphrodesia
Magic Garden Herb Co.
Rocky Hollow Herb Farm
KETCHUP/catsup
Deer Valley Farm
KEY lime pies
R. H. Chamberlin
KHOWLANJAN
Sahadi Import Co.
KINAKO
Katagiri
KINO root
Magic Garden Herb Co.
KIPPER snacks
Charlotte Charles, Inc.
KISHIMEN (shimodaya)
Katagiri
KISOBA (ninben)
Katagiri
KIZAMI surume
Katagiri
KIZAMIKOBU
Katagiri
KNOCKWURST
Schaller and Weber, Inc.
KNOTGRASS
Roth and Son
KOAJI
Katagiri
KOBU-ame
Katagiri
KOBUCHA
Katagiri

KOBUMAKI
Katagiri
KODAI
Katagiri
KOKUHO
Katagiri
KOLA nut
Magic Garden Herb Co.
KOLA nut powder
The Herb Lady
KOMPEITO
Katagiri
KOSHER products
Charlotte Charles, Inc.
KOSHIAN
Katagiri
KOTA
Old Town Natural Foods
KOUL weshkour, nut filled
Sahadi Import Co.
KOUMEZUKE
Katagiri
KOYADOFU
Katagiri
KUEMMEL kaese sticks
The Swiss Colony
KUMQUATS
Oriental Country Store
KUNSEI
Katagiri
KUROMAME
Katagiri
KYWII-no-kyuchan
Katagiri
LADY'S mantle
Aphrodesia
Lhasa Karnak Herb Co.
Rocky Hollow Herb Farm

LADY'S slipper
  Aphrodesia
LAKERDA, pickled fish
  Sahadi Import Co.
LAMB chops
  Omaha Steaks International
  Stock Yards Packing Co., Inc.
LAMB, leg of
  Stock Yards Packing Co., Inc.
LAMB roast seasoning
  Paprikas Weiss Importer
LAMB, smoked
  McArthur's Somkehouse, Inc.
LASAGNA, spinach
  Manganaro Foods
LAVENDER flowers
  Lhasa Karnak Herb Co.
  Old Town Natural Foods
  Paprikas Weiss Importer
  Rocky Hollow Herb Farm
  Roth and Son
LEEKS
  Aphrodesia
  Les Echalottes
LEMON balm
  Old Town Natural Foods
  Rocky Hollow Herb Farm
  Roth and Son
LEMON drops, Sicilian
  Paprikas Weiss Importer
LEMON marmalade
  Les Echalottes
LEMON peel
  Aphrodesia
  Paprikas Weiss Importer
LEMON peel, candied
  Paprikas Weiss Importer

LEMON peel, dried and candied
  Roth and Son
LEMON pickle
  Sahadi Import Co.
LEMONGRASS
  Aphrodesia
  Old Town Natural Foods
LEMONS
  Jaffe Bros. Natural Foods
LENTIL pilaf
  Sahadi Import Co.
LENTILS
  Deer Valley Farm
  Rocky Hollow Herb Farm
  Roth and Son
  Sahadi Import Co.
LENTILS, baked
  Manganaro Foods
LENTILS, red or green
  Paprikas Weiss Importer
LENTILS, red split
  Sahadi Import Co.
LICORICE candy (see Candy,
  licorice)
LICORICE chips
  Roth and Son
  Sahadi Import Co.
LICORICE drops
  Paprikas Weiss Importer
LICORICE root
  Aphrodesia
  Lhasa Karnak Herb Co.
  Magic Garden Herb Co.
  Oriental Country Store
  Paprikas Weiss Importer
  Rocky Hollow Herb Farm
  Roth and Son

LICORICE sticks
  Old Town Natural Foods
LIFE everlasting
  Aphrodesia
LIFE root
  Magic Garden Herb Co.
LILACS, crystallized
  Aphrodesia
LILI flower, dried
  Kam Shing Co.
LILY buds
  Aphrodesia
LILY of the valley leaves
  Aphrodesia
LIMA beans
  Deer Valley Farm
  Old Town Natural Foods
  Paprikas Weiss Importer
  Roth and Son
LIME marmalade
  Les Echalottes
  Roth and Son
LIME pickle
  Les Echalottes
  Sahadi Import Co.
LINDEN
  Empire Coffee and Tea Co
  Lhasa Karnak Herb Co.
  Old Town Natural Foods
  Rocky Hollow Herb Farm
LINZER tarts
  Paprikas Weiss Importer
LINZER tarts with ground almonds
  Les Echalottes
LIQUER mints
  The Swiss Colony

LIVER and bacon roll
  The Swiss Colony
LIVER pate (see Pates)
LIVER sausage
  The Swiss Colony
LOBELIA
  Aphrodesia
  Lhasa Karnak Herb Co.
  Magic Garden Herb Co.
  Old Town Natural Foods
  Rocky Hollow Herb Farm
LOBSTER
  Breman House, Inc.
  R. H. Chamberlin
  Charlotte Charles, Inc.
  Clambake International, Inc.
  Embassy Seafoods
  Omaha Steaks International
  Saltwater Farm
  Stock Yards Packing Co., Inc.
  The Swiss Colony
LOBSTER bisque
  Les Echalottes
LOBSTER paste
  Les Echalottes
LOBSTER souffle
  Les Echalottes
LOTUS
  Aphrodesia
LOTUS roots
  Rocky Hollow Herb Farm
LOTUS seeds
  Rocky Hollow Herb Farm
LOVAGE root
  Aphrodesia
  Magic Garden Herb Co.

LUBISC
  Manganaro Foods
LUCKY hand (salap root)
  Aphrodesia
LUPINI
  Sahadi Import Co.
LUPINI beans (see Beans, lupini)
LYCHEE nuts
  Kam Shing Co.
  Oriental Country Store
  Plantation Acres
  Rocky Hollow Herb Farm
LYCHEES
  Les Echalottes
LYCHEES in syrup
  Sahadi Import Co.
MACADAMIA nut cakes
  The Swiss Colony
MACADAMIA torte
  The Swiss Colony
MACADAMIAS
  Jaffe Bros. Natural Foods
  Kakawateez, Limited
  Les Echalottes
  Sahadi Import Co.
  The Swiss Colony
MACARONI (see also Noodles)
MACARONI, elbow
  Paprikas Weiss Importer
MACAROON, almond
  Les Echalottes
MACE
  Aphrodesia
  Lhasa Karnak Herb Co.
  Paprikas Weiss Importer
  Rocky Hollow Herb Farm
  Roth and Son

MACKEREL
  Manganaro Foods
MACKEREL fillet
  Sahadi Import Co.
MACKEREL marinated with wine
  Les Echalottes
MAHLAB
  Aphrodesia
  Sahadi Import Co.
MAIDENHAIR
  Aphrodesia
MAIMONE
  Manganaro Foods
MALLOW flower, black
  Roth and Son
MALVA
  Empire Coffee and Tea Co.
  Old Town Natural Foods
  Roth and Son
MALVA flowers
  Aphrodesia
MAMOUL, date filled
  Sahadi Import Co.
MAMOUL, pistachio filled
  Sahadi Import Co.
MAMOUL, walnut filled
  Sahadi Import Co.
MANDARIN orange slices in
  kirsch
  Paprikas Weiss Importer
MANDRAKE root
  Old Town Natural Foods
MANGO kasoondie (hot)
  Les Echalottes
MANGO pickle
  Les Echalottes
  Sahadi Import Co.

MANGO, sliced in syrup
  Sahadi Import Co.
MANGOS
  All Organics, Inc.
MANICOTTI, stuffed
  Manganaro Foods
MANTECHA, cheese
  Manganaro Foods
MAPLE candy (see Candy, maple)
MAPLE nut fudge
  The Swiss Colony
MAPLE syrup
  The Appleyard Corporation
  Charlotte Charles, Inc.
  Dakin Farm
  Deer Valley Farm
  Embassy Seafoods
  Sugarbush Farms, Inc.
  Watson, Peter and Tina
MARIGOLD flowers
  Aphrodesia
MARIGOLD petals
  Magic Garden Herb Co.
MARGARINE
  Deer Valley Farm
MARJORAM
  Aphrodesia
  Deer Valley Farm
  Lhasa Karnak Herb Co.
  Magic Garden Herb Co.
  Paprikas Weiss Importer
  Rocky Hollow Herb Farm
  Roth and Son
  Sahadi Import Co.
MARMALADE (see under specific
  type, e.g. Lemon marmalade,
  etc.)

MARMALADE, coarse cut
  Les Echalottes
MARMALADE, orange
  Les Echalottes
  Paprikas Weiss Importer
  Sahadi Import Co.
  The Swiss Colony
MARMALADE, Scotch whiskey
MARRON glaces
  Paprikas Weiss Importer
MARRON glaces, candied chestnut
  Les Echalottes
MARRONS (see also Chestnuts)
MARRONS, de puree—naturel
  Les Echalottes
MARRONS in syrup
  Les Echalottes
  Manganaro Foods
MARRONS in vanilla syrup
  Les Echalottes
MARSHMALLOW flowers
  Roth and Son
MARSHMALLOW leaves
  Roth and Son
MARSHMALLOW root
  Aphrodesia
  Roth and Son
MARSHMALLOWS
  Paprikas Weiss Importer
  The Swiss Colony
MARUBOSHI
  Katagiri
MARZIPAN
  Breman House, Inc.
  Charlotte Charles, Inc.
  Les Echalottes
  Roth and Son

MARZIPAN bars
  Paprikas Weiss Importer
MARZIPAN, Danish
  Paprikas Weiss Importer
MARZIPAN, potato
  Roth and Son
MARZIPAN tray
  The Swiss Colony
MASTIC
  Aphrodesia
  Rocky Hollow Herb Farm
MASTIC gum
  Sahadi Import Co.
MATE leaves
  Magic Garden Herb Co.
  Old Town Natural Foods
MATICO leaves
  Magic Garden Herb Co.
MAYONNAISE, kewpie
  Katagiri
MEAT (see also Beef, Pork, etc.)
MEAT ball seasoning
  Paprikas Weiss Importer
MEAT balls, cocktail
  Les Echalottes
MEAT products, European style
  Breman House, Inc.
MEAT tenderizer
  Paprikas Weiss Importer
MELON seeds
  Sahadi Import Co.
MELONS, sweet pickled
  Charlotte Charles, Inc.
MENMA
  Katagiri
MERINGUE powder
  Roth and Son

MIDORI-no-kaouri (sencha)
  Katagiri
MILK chocolate (see Chocolate, milk)
MILK, goat
  Diamond Dairy Goat Farm
MILK, powdered
  Deer Valley Farm
  Old Town Natural Foods
MILLET
  Old Town Natural Foods
  Rocky Hollow Herb Farm
MILLET seeds
  Paprikas Weiss Importer
  Roth and Son
MIMOSA
  Aphrodesia
MINCE pie, Old English
  Les Echalottes
MINCEMEAT with brandy
  Les Echalottes
MINERAL water, Amaro
  Manganaro Foods
MINERAL water, Bitterino
  Manganaro Foods
MINERAL water, Chinotto
  Manganaro Foods
MINERAL water, ginger
  Manganaro Foods
MINERAL water, lemon
  Manganaro Foods
MINERAL water, orange
  Manganaro Foods
MINESTRONE (see Soup)
MINT
  Kalustyan
  Paprikas Weiss Importer

Sahadi Import Co.
Victoria Packing Corp.
MINT cakes
Les Echalottes
MINT candy (see Candy, mint)
MINT honey
The Swiss Colony
MINT jelly
Les Echalottes
MINT leaves
Aphrodesia
MINT lentils
Sahadi Import Co.
MINT toffee
The Swiss Colony
MINT torte
The Swiss Colony
MINTS, butter (see Butter mints)
MINTS, chocolate (see Chocolate
mints)
MIRA lemon pickle
Sahadi Import Co.
MIRINBOSHI iwashi
Katagiri
MISTLETOE
Aphrodesia
Magic Garden Herb Co.
MIZUYOKAN
Katagiri
MLOUKHUJEH
Sahadi Import Co.
MOCHIGOME
Katagiri
MOCHIKO
Katagiri
MOGHRABIYCH
Sahadi Import Co.

MOLASSES
Deer Valley Farm
MOLASSES, grape
Sahadi Import Co.
MOLASSES, West Indian
Roth and Son
MONAKA-no-kawa
Katagiri
MONG dall
Sahadi Import Co.
MORILLES
Les Echalottes
MORTADELLA
Manganaro Foods
The Swiss Colony
MOSTARDA
Manganaro Foods
MOTHERWORT
Aphrodesia
Magic Garden Herb Co.
Old Town Natural Foods
MUFFINS
Deer Valley Farm
MUGICHA
Katagiri
MUGWORT
Aphrodesia
Lhasa Karnak Herb Co.
Paprikas Weiss Importer
Rocky Hollow Herb Farm
Roth and Son
MUIRAPUAMA bark
Magic Garden Herb Co.
MULLEIN
Aphrodesia
MULLEIN flowers
Rocky Hollow Herb Farm

MULLEIN leaves
  Magic Garden Herb Co.
  Rocky Hollow Herb Farm
MUNG beans (see Beans, mung)
MURCOTTS
  R. H. Chamberlin
MUSHROOM powder
  Paprikas Weiss Importer
MUSHROOMS
  Aphrodesia
  Breman House, Inc.
  Charlotte Charles, Inc.
  Manganaro Foods
  Sahadi Import Co.
  Victoria Packing Corp.
MUSHROOMS—cepes—naturel
  Manganaro Foods
MUSHROOMS, dried
  Manganaro Foods
  Paprikas Weiss Importer
MUSHROOMS, dried (Chinese)
  Oriental Country Store
MUSHROOMS, freeze dried
  Les Echalottes
MUSHROOMS, mixed
  Paprikas Weiss Importer
MUSHROOMS, risotto
  Manganaro Foods
MUSHROOMS, stone
  Paprikas Weiss Importer
MUSHROOMS, wild
  Paprikas Weiss Importer

MUSK crystals
  Aphrodesia
MUSK root
  Aphrodesia
  Magic Garden Herb Co.

MUSSELS
  Charlotte Charles, Inc.
  Les Echalottes
  Manganaro Foods
MUSSELS fried in butter
  Les Echalottes
MUSSELS, marinated
  Manganaro Foods
MUSSELS on half shell
  Les Echalottes
MUSTARD
  Deer Valley Farm
  Katagiri
  Victoria Packing Corp.
MUSTARD, English
  Les Echalottes
  Paprikas Weiss Importer
MUSTARD, French
  Les Echalottes
  Manganaro Foods
MUSTARD, green, preserved
  Kam Shing Co.
MUSTARD, green, salted
  Kam Shing Co.
MUSTARD oil
  Sahadi Import Co.
MUSTARD powder
  Aphrodesia
MUSTARD seed
  Paprikas Weiss Importer
  Roth and Son
MUSTARD seeds, black
  Aphrodesia
  Rocky Hollow Herb Farm
MUSTARD seeds, yellow
  Aphrodesia
  Rocky Hollow Herb Farm

MUSTARD, tricoulor Orleans
  Les Echalottes
MUSTARD, Viennese style
  Paprikas Weiss Importer
MYRRH
  Aphrodesia
  Old Town Natural Foods
MYRRH gum
  Magic Garden Herb Co.
NAGASAKI chanpon
  Katagiri
NAMAWAKAME
  Katagiri
NAMETAKE ajitsuke
  Katagiri
NARAZUKE
  Katagiri
NARAZUKE (chuyu)
  Katagiri
NARAZUKE (kyuri)
  Katagiri
NARAZUKE (uri)
  Katagiri
NASI goreng
  Les Echalottes
NECTARINES, dried
  Sahadi Import Co.
NETTLE
  Aphrodesia
  Old Town Natural Foods
NETTLE leaves
  Magic Garden Herb Co.
NETTLE, stinging
  Rocky Hollow Herb Farm
NEWBERRY seasoning
  Paprikas Weiss Importer
NEWBURG sauce
  Embassy Seafoods

NIHON su (mitsukan)
  Katagiri
NIKKE senbei
  Katagiri
NISHIMEKOBU
  Katagiri
NONPARIEL seed
  Roth and Son
NOODLES, buckwheat
  Chico-San, Inc.
  Old Town Natural Foods
NOODLES, egg
  Kam Shing Co.
  Manganaro Foods
  Roth and Son
NOODLES, green
  Manganaro Foods
NOODLES, home-made
  Manganaro Foods
NOODLES, macaroni
  Deer Valley Farm
NOODLES, spaghetti
  Deer Valley Farm
NOODLES, spinach
  Charlotte Charles, Inc.
  Manganaro Foods
NOODLES, whole wheat
  Chico-San, Inc.
  Old Town Natural Foods
NORI/ajitsuke (yamagataya)
  Katagiri
NORI fumi
  Katagiri
NORI furikane
  Katagiri
NORI senbei
  Katagiri

NORI tamago
  Katagiri
NORI tsukudani
  Katagiri
NUKA
  Katagiri
NUKAMISO-no-moto
  Katagiri
NUT loaves
  Charlotte Charles, Inc.
NUTMEG
  Aphrodesia
  Deer Valley Farm
  Lhasa Karnak Herb Co.
  Magic Garden Herb Co.
  Paprikas Weiss Importer
  Rocky Hollow Herb Farm
  Roth and Son
  Sahadi Import Co.
NUTS (see under specific type, e.g.
    Brazil nuts, Pignolia nuts, etc.)
  Bailey's of Boston, Inc.
  Catherine's Chocolate Shop
  Charlotte Charles, Inc.
  Deer Valley Farm
NUTS, mixed
  Sahadi Import Co.
  The Swiss Colony
NUTTY crunch
  The Swiss Colony
OAK bark, red
  Rocky Hollow Herb Farm
OAK moss
  Aphrodesia
OAT flakes, rolled
  Rocky Hollow Herb Farm
OAT flour (see Flour, oat)

OATMEAL
  Charlotte Charles, Inc.
  Deer Valley Farm
OATMEAL cookies (see Cookies,
    oatmeal)
OATMEAL, Irish
  Paprikas Weiss Importer
OATMEAL, Scotch style
  Paprikas Weiss Importer
OATMEAL, steel cut
  Paprikas Weiss Importer
  Roth and Son
OBOROKOBU
  Katagiri
OCHAZUKENORI
  Katagiri
OCTOPUS
  Charlotte Charles, Inc.
OKAKA
  Katagiri
OKONOMIYAKI
  Katagiri
OKONOMIZUKE shoga
  Katagiri
OKOSHI
  Katagiri
OKRA
  Sahadi Import Co.
OKRA, baby
  Sahadi Import Co.
OKRA with tomatoes
  Sahadi Import Co.
OIL, peanut, pure
  Les Echalottes
OIL, salad
  Sahadi Import Co.

OIL, sesame
Aphrodesia
Chico-San, Inc.
Kam Shing Co.
Oriental Country Store
OIL, sesame (goma)
Katagiri
OIL, sesame (seerij)
Sahadi Import Co.
OIL, tahini
Sahadi Import Co.
OIL, walnut
Les Echalottes
Paprikas Weiss Importer
OILS, vegetable
Deer Valley Farm
OLIVE oil
Sahadi Import Co.
OLIVE oil, French
Les Echalottes
OLIVES
Charlotte Charles, Inc.
Victoria Packing Corp.
OLIVES, black
Sahadi Import Co.
OLIVES, Calarnata
Manganaro Foods
OLIVES, gaeta
Manganaro Foods
OLIVES, green
Sahadi Import Co.
OLIVES, plain ripe, Italy
Manganaro Foods
OLIVES, Spanish
Manganaro Foods
OMELET
The Swiss Colony

ONION cheese ball
The Swiss Colony
ONION flakes
Paprikas Weiss Importer
Rocky Hollow Herb Farm
Roth and Son
ONION, minced
Paprikas Weiss Importer
ONION powder
Aphrodesia
Empire Coffee and Tea Co.
Paprikas Weiss Importer
Rocky Hollow Herb Farm
Roth and Son
ONION salt
Rocky Hollow Herb Farm
Roth and Son
ONION soup and dip mix
Paprikas Weiss Importer
ONIONS
Charlotte Charles, Inc.
ONIONS, chopped
Aphrodesia
ONIONS, fried
Les Echalottes
ONIONS, pickled
Charlotte Charles, Inc.
ORANGE blossoms
Aphrodesia
Old Town Natural Foods
Rocky Hollow Herb Farm
ORANGE cordial cake
The Swiss Colony
ORANGE flavoring
Paprikas Weiss Importer
ORANGE flower essence
Paprikas Weiss Importer

ORANGE flower water
  Les Echalottes
  Sahadi Import Co.
ORANGE nut cake
  The Swiss Colony
ORANGE peel
  Aphrodesia
  Paprikas Weiss Importer
  Roth and Son
ORANGE peel, candied
  Paprikas Weiss Importer
  Roth and Son
ORANGE peel, hot pickle
  Les Echalottes
ORANGE segments
  Charlotte Charles, Inc.
ORANGE slices (see also
    Mandarin orange slices)
  Paprikas Weiss Importer
ORANGES
  Jaffe Bros. Natural Foods
  The Swiss Colony
ORANGES, fresh
  Deer Valley Farm
ORANGES, navel
  R. H. Chamberlin
  Lee's Fruit Co., Inc.
  Pavone Ranch
ORANGES, satsuma
  Lee's Fruit Co., Inc.
ORANGES, temple
  R. H. Chamberlin
  Lee's Fruit Co., Inc.
ORANGES, valencia
  R. H. Chamberlin
  Pavone Ranch

OREGANO
  Aphrodesia
  Deer Valley Farm
  Lhasa Karnak Herb Co.
  Paprikas Weiss Importer
  Rocky Hollow Herb Farm
  Roth and Son
  Victoria Packing Corp.
OREGANO leaves
  Magic Garden Herb Co.
ORRIS root
  Aphrodesia
  Rocky Hollow Herb Farm
  Roth and Son
OSHIMUGI
  Katagiri
OSTYPKA
  Paprikas Weiss Importer
OXTAIL consomme
  Paprikas Weiss Importer
OYSTERS
  Charlotte Charles, Inc.
OYSTERS, smoked
  Les Echalottes
  Manganaro Foods
  Sahadi Import Co.
PAINSOL
  Les Echalottes
PALM (see Hearts of palm)
PALM leaves
  Les Echalottes
PANCAKE mixes
  Charlotte Charles, Inc.
  Deer Valley Farm
  Paprikas Weiss Importer
  The Swiss Colony

PANCETTA
  Manganaro Foods
PANDORO
  Manganaro Foods
PANETTONE
  Manganaro Foods
PANFORTE
  Manganaro Foods
PANKO
  Katagiri
PAPAYA
  Deer Valley Farm
  Manganaro Foods
  Rocky Hollow Herb Farm
PAPAYA leaves
  Aphrodesia
  Magic Garden Herb Co.
  Old Town Natural Foods
PAPPADUMS
  Sahadi Import Co.
PAPPADUMS wafers
  Les Echalottes
PAPRIKA
  Aphrodesia
  Charlotte Charles, Inc.
  Lhasa Karnak Herb Co.
  Paprikas Weiss Importer
  Rocky Hollow Herb Farm
  Roth and Son
  Sahadi Import Co.
  Victoria Packing Corp.
PARSLEY
  Aphrodesia
  Deer Valley Farm
  Lhasa Karnak Herb Co.
  Rocky Hollow Herb Farm
  Victoria Packing Corp.

PARSLEY flakes
  Paprikas Weiss Importer
  Roth and Son
PASSION flower
  Aphrodesia
  The Herb Lady
  Lhasa Karnak Herb Co.
  Magic Garden Herb Co.
  Old Town Natural Foods
  Rocky Hollow Herb Farm
PASTA (see also under specific
      type, e.g., Bow ties, Noodle
      etc.)
PASTA, all brands
  Manganaro Foods
PASTA barilla
  Manganaro Foods
PASTA con sarde
  Manganaro Foods
PASTA fagiola
  Manganaro Foods
PASTENE
  Manganaro Foods
PASTILLES, chocolate
  Paprikas Weiss Importer
PASTILLES, raspberry, stra
    honey
  Roth and Son
PATCHOULY
  Paprikas Weiss Importer
  Roth and Son
PATCHOULY leaves
  Aphrodesia
  Magic Garden Herb Co.
  Rocky Hollow Herb Farm
PATES (many exotic varieties, to
    complicated to list)

Charlotte Charles, Inc.
Les Echalottes
Manganaro Foods
Paprikas Weiss Importer
Roth and Son
The Swiss Colony
PATKO
Paprikas Weiss Importer
PAWA, rice flakes
Sahadi Import Co.
PEA beans
Paprikas Weiss Importer
Rocky Hollow Herb Farm
PEACH kernels
Rocky Hollow Herb Farm
PEACH leaves
Aphrodesia
Rocky Hollow Herb Farm
PEACH seeds
Aphrodesia
PEACHES
Victoria Packing Corp.
PEACHES, dried
Roth and Son
Sahadi Import Co.
PEACHES, glazed
Sahadi Import Co.
PEACHES, prepared
Charlotte Charles, Inc.
Deer Valley Farm
PEACHES, preserved
Paprikas Weiss Importer
PEACHES, sundried
Rocky Hollow Herb Farm
PEANUT brittle
Catherine's Chocolate Shop

PEANUT butter
Deer Valley Farm
L. & L. Health Foods Co.
PEANUTS
Rocky Hollow Herb Farm
The Swiss Colony
PEANUTS, chocolate
Paprikas Weiss Importer
PEANUTS, raw
Deer Valley Farm
L. & L. Health Foods Co.
Oriental Country Store
PEANUTS, roasted
Deer Valley Farm
Kakawateez, Limited
PEANUTS, salted
Bailey's of Boston, Inc.
The Packing Shed
PEANUTS, Spanish
Jaffe Bros. Natural Foods
PEANUTS, toasted in butter
The Swiss Colony
PEAR flavoring
Paprikas Weiss Importer
PEARS
Victoria Packing Corp.
PEARS, candied in pear liquer
Paprikas Weiss Importer
PEARS, comice
The Swiss Colony
PEARS, dried
Sahadi Import Co.
PEARS, dried and candied
Roth and Son
PEARS, glazed
Sahadi Import Co.

PEARS, sundried
    Rocky Hollow Herb Farm
PEAS
    Charlotte Charles, Inc.
    Deer Valley Farm
    Manganaro Foods
    Roth and Son
PEAS, split
    Deer Valley Farm
    Paprikas Weiss Importer
    Rocky Hollow Herb Farm
PECAN brittle
    Priester's Pecans
PECAN-cheddar wheel
    The Swiss Colony
PECAN cheese ball
    The Swiss Colony
PECAN pound cake
    The Swiss Colony
PECANS
    Bailey's of Boston, Inc.
    Breakfast Creek Farm
    Charlotte Charles, Inc.
    Deer Valley Farm
    Jaffe Bros. Natural Foods
    Koinonia Products
    L. & L. Health Foods Co.
    Paprikas Weiss Importer
    Plumridge
    Priester's Pecans
    Rocky Hollow Herb Farm
    Sternberg Pecan Company
    Young Pecan Sales Corp.
PECTIN
    Roth and Son

PENNYROYAL
    Aphrodesia
    Old Town Natural Foods
    Rocky Hollow Herb Farm
PEONY root
    Aphrodesia
PEPATO, cheese
    Manganaro Foods
PEPERONATA
    Paprikas Weiss Importer
PEPPER
    Rocky Hollow Herb Farm
PEPPER, black
    Empire Coffee and Tea Co.
    Lhasa Karnak Herb Co.
    Paprikas Weiss Importer
    Roth and Son
    Victoria Packing Corp.
PEPPER, creole
    Paprikas Weiss Importer
PEPPER, house
    Katagiri
PEPPER, red hot
    Sahadi Import Co.
PEPPER spice corn
    Kam Shing Co.
PEPPER, Szechuan
    Aphrodesia
    Roth and Son
PEPPER, white
    Empire Coffee and Tea Co.
    Lhasa Karnak Herb Co.
    Paprikas Weiss Importer
    Roth and Son
PEPPERCORNS
    Aphrodesia
    Paprikas Weiss Importer

PEPPERCORNS, green
  Aphrodesia
PEPPERMINT
  Aphrodesia
  Empire Coffee and Tea Co.
  The Herb Lady
  Lhasa Karnak Herb Co.
  Magic Garden Herb Co.
  Old Town Natural Foods
  Rocky Hollow Herb Farm
PEPPERMINT drops
  Roth and Son
PEPPERMINT leaves
  Paprikas Weiss Importer
PEPPERMINTS, French
  Roth and Son
PEPPERMINTS, German
  Paprikas Weiss Importer
PEPPERONCINI
  Victoria Packing Corp.
PEPPERONI
  Manganaro Foods
PEPPERS, antipasto
  Victoria Packing Corp.
PEPPERS, fried
  Victoria Packing Corp.
PEPPERS, jalapeno
  Charlotte Charles, Inc.
PEPPERS, pickled
  Sahadi Import Co.
PEPPERS, red and yellow
  Les Echalottes
  Manganaro Foods
  Paprikas Weiss Importer
PEPPERS, roasted
  Manganaro Foods
  Victoria Packing Corp.

PEPPERS, stuffed
  Paprikas Weiss Importer
  Sahadi Import Co.
  Victoria Packing Corp.
PEPPERS, stuffed, cherry
  Manganaro Foods
PEPPERS, sweet, flakes
  Paprikas Weiss Importer
PERIWINKLE
  Aphrodesia
  Lhasa Karnak Herb Co.
  Rocky Hollow Herb Farm
PESTO alla Genovese
  Manganaro Foods
PETIT beurre
  Les Echalottes
  The Swiss Colony
PETIT fours
  Charlotte Charles, Inc.
  The Swiss Colony
PETIT pois
  Paprikas Weiss Importer
PHEASANT
  Omaha Steaks International
PHEASANT, smoked
  The Forsts
  The Swiss Colony
PICKLES (see also under specific
    type, e.g. Lemon pickles,
    Gherkins, etc.)
  Kalustyan
PICKLES, dill
  Charlotte Charles, Inc.
  Deer Valley Farm
  Victoria Packing Corp.
PICKLES, ding how
  Kam Shing Co.

PICKLES, German
Breman House, Inc.
PICKLES, kosher
Victoria Packing Corp.
PICKLES, sour
Victoria Packing Corp.
PICKLES, sweet
Charlotte Charles, Inc.
Victoria Packing Corp.
PICKLING spice
Aphrodesia
Paprikas Weiss Importer
PIE/pastry shells
Charlotte Charles, Inc.
PIES, apple
Deer Valley Farm
PIES, pineapple
Deer Valley Farm
PIES, pumpkin
Deer Valley Farm
PIGEON peas
Paprikas Weiss Importer
PIGNOLIA nuts
Aphrodesia
Manganaro Foods
Paprikas Weiss Importer
Rocky Hollow Herb Farm
Sahadi Import Co.
PIGS' ears
Victoria Packing Corp.
PIGS' feet
Victoria Packing Corp.
PIGS' knuckles
Victoria Packing Corp.
PIGS' snouts
Victoria Packing Corp.
PIGS' tails
Victoria Packing Corp.

PIKE dumplings naturel
Les Echalottes
PILAF (see under specific type, e.g
Lentil pilaf, etc.)
PIMENTOS
Manganaro Foods
PINE nuts (see Pignolia nuts)
PINE resin
Magic Garden Herb Co.
PINEAPPLE
Charlotte Charles, Inc.
Rocky Hollow Herb Farm
The Swiss Colony
PINEAPPLE, candied
Paprikas Weiss Importer
Roth and Son
PINEAPPLE products
Deer Valley Farm
PINEAPPLES, imported, sundried
Sahadi Import Co.
PINTO beans (see Beans, pinto)

PIPING gel
Roth and Son
PIPSISSEWA
Aphrodesia
PISTACHIO fingers
Sahadi Import Co.
PISTACHIOS
Kakawateez, Limited
Paprikas Weiss Importer
Rocky Hollow Herb Farm
Sahadi Import Co.
The Swiss Colony
PISTACHIOS, sugar coated
Sahadi Import Co.
PIZZA
The Swiss Colony

PIZZA seasoning
  Paprikas Weiss Importer
PLANTAIN
  Aphrodesia
  Old Town Natural Foods
PLEURISY root
  Aphrodesia
  Roth and Son
PLUM butter
  Roth and Son
PLUMS, dried, in armagnac
  Paprikas Weiss Importer
PLUMS, prepared
  Charlotte Charles, Inc.
  Chico-San, Inc.
POCAN bush
  Magic Garden Herb Co.
POIVRE aromatique
  Paprikas Weiss Importer
POKE root
  Aphrodesia
POLENTA, instant
  Les Echalottes
  Manganaro Foods
POMANDER
  Aphrodesia
POMEGRANATE seeds
  Aphrodesia
  Rocky Hollow Herb Farm
PONZU
  Katagiri
POPCORN
  Deer Valley Farm
  L. & L. Health Foods Co.
  Old Town Natural Foods
  Roth and Son
POPCORN, honey caramel
  The Swiss Colony

POPPY flowers
  Aphrodesia
  Rocky Hollow Herb Farm
POPPY seed filling
  Paprikas Weiss Importer
POPPY seeds
  Aphrodesia
  Lhasa Karnak Herb Co.
  Paprikas Weiss Importer
  Rocky Hollow Herb Farm
  Sahadi Import Co.
PORK barbeque
  Smithfield Ham and Products
    Co., Inc.
PORK chops
  Omaha Steaks International
  Stock Yards Packing Co., Inc.
POTASH
  Paprikas Weiss Importer
  Roth and Son
POTATO pancake mix
  Paprikas Weiss Importer
POTATO starch
  Roth and Son
POTATOES
  Breman House, Inc.
  Charlotte Charles, Inc.
POTPOURRI
  Magic Garden Herb Co.
POULTRY/game
  Breman House, Inc.
  Charlotte Charles, Inc.
POULTRY/game, rock Cornish
    hens
  The Swiss Colony
POULTRY seasoning
  Paprikas Weiss Importer
  Roth and Son

POUND cake flavoring
  Paprikas Weiss Importer
PRALINES
  Charlotte Charles, Inc.
  Priester's Pecans
PREPARED meals, Hungarian
  Charlotte Charles, Inc.
PREPARED meals, Italian
  Charlotte Charles, Inc.
PREPARED meals, Swedish
  Charlotte Charles, Inc.
PRESERVES (see also Jams/
    jellies/preserves)
PRESERVES, gooseberry
  Les Echalottes
  Paprikas Weiss Importer
  Roth and Son
PRESERVES, imported fruit
  Breman House, Inc.
PRESERVES, Jamaica mango
    and ginger
  Roth and Son
PRESERVES, lingon berry
  Roth and Son
PRESERVES, raspberry
  Les Echalottes
PRESERVES, red currant
  Les Echalottes
PRESERVES, sour cherry
  Les Echalottes
PRESERVES, strawberry
  Les Echalottes
PRIMROSE
  Aphrodesia
PROSCUITTINO
  Manganaro Foods
PROSCUITTO
  Manganaro Foods

PRUNE butter
  Paprikas Weiss Importer
  Roth and Son
PRUNE flavoring
  Paprikas Weiss Importer
PRUNES
  Charlotte Charles, Inc.
  L. & L. Health Foods Co.
  The Swiss Colony
PRUNES, dried and candied
  Roth and Son
PRUNES, imported, natural
  Sahadi Import Co.
PRUNES, sundried
  Rocky Hollow Herb Farm
PSYLLIUM seeds
  Aphrodesia
PUDDING, chocolate with almond
  Paprikas Weiss Importer
PUDDING, cream, powder
  Paprikas Weiss Importer
PUDDING, currant sponge
  Les Echalottes
PUDDING, date sponge
  Les Echalottes
PUDDING, Dijon
  Les Echalottes
PUDDING, English sponge
  Les Echalottes
PUDDING, ginger sponge
  Les Echalottes
PUDDING, golden syrup sponge
  Les Echalottes
PUDDING, marmalade sponge
  Les Echalottes
PUDDING, mixed fruit sponge
  Les Echalottes
PUDDING, plum
  Les Echalottes

PUDDING powder, almond
  Paprikas Weiss Importer
PUDDING powder, caramel
  Paprikas Weiss Importer
PUDDING powder, chocolate
  Paprikas Weiss Importer
PUDDING powder, lemon
  Paprikas Weiss Importer
PUDDING powder, "Mandella"
  Paprikas Weiss Importer
PUDDING powder, raspberry
  Paprikas Weiss Importer
PUDDING powder, strawberry
  Paprikas Weiss Importer
PUDDING, sultana sponge
  Les Echalottes
PUDDINGS/pudding mixes
  Breman House, Inc.
  Charlotte Charles, Inc.
PUFFS
  Charlotte Charles, Inc.
PUMPERNICKEL bread
  Breman House, Inc.
  Charlotte Charles, Inc.
  Paprikas Weiss Importer
PUMPERNICKEL bread mix
  Paprikas Weiss Importer
PUMPKIN
  Deer Valley Farm
PUMPKIN pie spice
  Paprikas Weiss Importer
PUMPKIN seeds
  Chico-San, Inc.
  Deer Valley Farm
  L. & L. Health Foods Co.
  Old Town Natural Foods
  Rocky Hollow Herb Farm

Roth and Son
Sahadi Import Co.
Victoria Packing Corp.
QUAIL
  Omaha Steaks International
QUASSIA chips
  Aphrodesia
  Magic Garden Herb Co.
QUATRE epices (French spice
  mix)
  Roth and Son
QUEEN of the meadow
  Aphrodesia
  Rocky Hollow Herb Farm
QUINCE, glazed, Australian
  Sahadi Import Co.
QUININE bark
  Aphrodesia
QUONG hop ben cake
  Kam Shing Co.
RABBIT (see Hare)
RADISH, preserved
  Kam Shing Co.
RAHAT locoum
  Sahadi Import Co.
RAINBOW torte
  Paprikas Weiss Importer
RAISINS
  L. & L. Health Foods Co.
  Rocky Hollow Herb Farm
  Sahadi Import Co.
RAISINS, chocolate
  Paprikas Weiss Importer
RAISINS, dried and candied
  Roth and Son
RAISINS, natural
  Sahadi Import Co.

164

RAISINS, white
  Paprikas Weiss Importer
RAKKYO
  Katagiri
RASPBERRIES
  Deer Valley Farm
  Plumridge
RASPBERRIES, dried
  Aphrodesia
  Roth and Son
RASPBERRIES, fancy
  Roth and Son
RASPBERRY drops
  Paprikas Weiss Importer
RASPBERRY flavoring
  Paprikas Weiss Importer
RASPBERRY leaves
  Aphrodesia
  Lhasa Karnak Herb Co.
  Magic Garden Herb Co.
  Old Town Natural Foods
  Rocky Hollow Herb Farm
RATATOUILLE
  Manganaro Foods
  Paprikas Weiss Importer
RATE grutze pudding powder
  Paprikas Weiss Importer
RAVIOLI
  Manganaro Foods
RAVIOLI with meat
  Paprikas Weiss Importer
RAYNAL and roquelaure
  Les Echalottes
RELISHES
  Deer Valley Farm
RICE (see also under specific
      type, e.g. Besmati rice)

Kalustyan
Roth and Son
RICE, arborio
  Manganaro Foods
RICE, brown
  Chico-San, Inc.
  Deer Valley Farm
  L. & L. Health Foods Co.
  Old Town Natural Foods
  Paprikas Weiss Importer
  Rocky Hollow Herb Farm
  Sahadi Import Co.
RICE cakes (see Cakes, rice)
RICE candy (see Candy, rice)
RICE flour (see Flour, rice)
RICE, Italian
  Deer Valley Farm
RICE paper wafer sheet
  Roth and Son
RICE pilaf
  Sahadi Import Co.
RICE seasoning
  Paprikas Weiss Importer
RICE stick
  Kam Shing Co.
RICE, sweet
  Chico-San, Inc.
  Kam Shing Co.
  Old Town Natural Foods
RICE, white
  Charlotte Charles, Inc.
RICE, wild
  Charlotte Charles, Inc.
  Deer Valley Farm
  Paprikas Weiss Importer
RISOTTO, Milanese
  Manganaro Foods

ROASTS, rib
  Stock Yards Packing Co.
ROASTS, sirloin
  Stock Yards Packing Co.
ROASTS, tenderloin
  Stock Yards Packing Co.
ROCK candy
  Aphrodesia
  Roth and Son
  Sahadi Import Co.
ROE
  Embassy Seafoods
ROLLMOPS
  Roth and Son
ROMAN beans
  Paprikas Weiss Importer
ROSA marina
  Sahadi Import Co.
ROSE, California blue
  Katagiri
ROSE jam
  Paprikas Weiss Importer
ROSE petals in syrup
  Paprikas Weiss Importer
ROSE water
  Aphrodesia
  Les Echalottes
  Roth and Son
  Sahadi Import Co.
ROSEBUDS
  Aphrodesia
  Old Town Natural Foods
  Rocky Hollow Herb Farm
  Roth and Son
ROSEHIPS
  Lhasa Karnak Herb Co.
  Magic Garden Herb Co.
  Old Town Natural Foods

Paprikas Weiss Importer
  Rocky Hollow Herb Farm
  Roth and Son
ROSEMARY
  Aphrodesia
  Deer Valley Farm
  Lhasa Karnak Herb Co.
  Magic Garden Herb Co.
  Rocky Hollow Herb Farm
  Roth and Son
ROSEMARY leaves
  Paprikas Weiss Importer
  Sahadi Import Co.
ROSES, crystallized
  Aphrodesia
ROSEWOOD powder
  Aphrodesia
ROULADE
  Paprikas Weiss Importer
ROULADE of ham
  Les Echalottes
RUE
  Aphrodesia
  Old Town Natural Foods
  Rocky Hollow Herb Farm
RUM babas (see Babas, rum)
RUM beans
  Roth and Son
RUM cakes (see Cakes, rum; also
      Babas, rum)
RUM flavored chocolate bottles
  Paprikas Weiss Importer
RUM flavoring
  Paprikas Weiss Importer
RUM sauce (see Sauce, rum)
RUM torte
  Paprikas Weiss Importer

RUM truffle
  Roth and Son
RYE berries
  Rocky Hollow Herb Farm
RYE flavoring
  Paprikas Weiss Importer
RYE flour (see Flour, rye)
RYOKOUME (satozuke)
  Katagiri
SACHER torte
  Paprikas Weiss Importer
SACHET
  Roth and Son
SAFFLOWER
  Aphrodesia
  Rocky Hollow Herb Farm
SAFFRON
  Aphrodesia
  Charlotte Charles, Inc.
  Lhasa Karnak Herb Co.
  Manganaro Foods
  Paprikas Weiss Importer
  Rocky Hollow Herb Farm
  Roth and Son
  Sahadi Import Co.
SAGE
  Aphrodesia
  Deer Valley Farm
  Lhasa Karnak Herb Co.
  Magic Garden Herb Co.
  Rocky Hollow Herb Farm
  Roth and Son
SAGE leaves
  Paprikas Weiss Importer
SAGE, red
  Old Town Natural Foods
SAGO
  Roth and Son

SAHLAB
  Sahadi Import Co.
SAINT John's wort
  Aphrodesia
  Rocky Hollow Herb Farm
SAKI-ika ajitsuke
  Katagiri
SAKURA denbu
  Katagiri
SAKURAEBI
  Katagiri
SALAD dressing, Irish
  Les Echalottes
SALAD dressing seasoning
  Paprikas Weiss Importer
SALAD dressings
  Deer Valley Farm
  De Sousa's—The Healthians
SALAD herb mix
  Roth and Son
SALAD usuyaki arare
  Katagiri
SALAMI
  The Forsts
  Manganaro Foods
  Schaller and Weber, Inc.
SALAMI, all beef
  Les Echalottes
SALAMI alla cacciatora
  Manganaro Foods
SALAMI, citterio
  Manganaro Foods
SALAMI, cocktail
  Les Echalottes
SALAMI, Hungarian
  Paprikas Weiss Importer
SALICYL
  Roth and Son

SALMON/salmon products
Breman House, Inc.
Charlotte Charles, Inc.
Embassy Seafoods
Omaha Steaks International
Ritchie Bros.
Saltwater Farm
SALMON kasuzuke
Katagiri
SALMON, salted
Katagiri
SALMON, sliced, smoked
Les Echalottes
SALONICA beans, white
Sahadi Import Co.
SALSIFY
Les Echalottes
Manganaro Foods
Paprikas Weiss Importer
SALT (see also under specific type,
e.g. Hickory smoke salt, etc.)
SALT, crystal
Paprikas Weiss Importer
SALT, sea
Les Echalottes
Roth and Son
SALTPETER
Roth and Son
SALTS
Aphrodesia
Charlotte Charles, Inc.
Chico-San, Inc.
Deer Valley Farm
SANDALWOOD
Aphrodesia
Magic Garden Herb Co.
SANICLE leaves
Old Town Natural Foods
Rocky Hollow Herb Farm

SANSHO powder
Katagiri
SARDINES/sardine products
Charlotte Charles, Inc.
Embassy Seafoods
Les Echalottes
Manganaro Foods
Roth and Son
Sahadi Import Co.
SARDINES, parodi
Manganaro Foods
SARSAPARILLA bark
The Herb Lady
SARSAPARILLA root
Aphrodesia
The Herb Lady
Lhasa Karnak Herb Co.
Magic Garden Herb Co.
Old Town Natural Foods
Rocky Hollow Herb Farm
SASAKAREI hoshi
Katagiri
SASHIMI shoyu
Katagiri
SASSAFRAS
Aphrodesia
Rocky Hollow Herb Farm
SASSAFRAS bark
Lhasa Karnak Herb Co.
Old Town Natural Foods
Roth and Son
SAUCE (see also under specific
type, e.g., Soy sauce, Spa-
ghetti sauce, etc.)
SAUCE, bean
Oriental Country Store
SAUCE Cumberland
Les Echalottes

SAUCE diable
  Les Echalottes
SAUCE, hard
  Les Echalottes
SAUCE, hoisin
  Kam Shing Co.
SAUCE, Hollandaise, mix
  Paprikas Weiss Importer
SAUCE, homard
  Les Echalottes
SAUCE, hunter, mix
  Paprikas Weiss Importer
SAUCE, ikari
  Katagiri
SAUCE, Irish mushroom
  Les Echalottes
SAUCE, kagome
  Katagiri
SAUCE, kagome tonkatsu
  Katagiri
SAUCE, madiera
  Les Echalottes
SAUCE melba
  Les Echalottes
SAUCE, mushroom, mix
  Paprikas Weiss Importer
SAUCE, nantua
  Les Echalottes
SAUCE, oyster
  Oriental Country Store
SAUCE, periguex
  Les Echalottes
SAUCE, plum
  Kam Shing Co.
SAUCE powder, vanilla
  Paprikas Weiss Importer
SAUCE, rairgote
  Les Echalottes

SAUCE Robert
  Les Echalottes
SAUCE, rum
  Les Echalottes
SAUCE, steak and chop
  Les Echalottes
SAUCE, white, mix
  Paprikas Weiss Importer
SAUERKRAUT (see also Sausage
    with sauerkraut)
  Breman House, Inc.
  Charlotte Charles, Inc.
  Deer Valley Farm
  Les Echalottes
  Victoria Packing Corp.
SAUSAGE (see also Knockwurst)
SAUSAGE, blood and tongue
  Schaller and Weber, Inc.
SAUSAGE, caraway
  The Swiss Colony
SAUSAGE, Hungarian
  Paprikas Weiss Importer
SAUSAGE, link, imported
  The Swiss Colony
SAUSAGE, ring
  Schaller and Weber, Inc.
SAUSAGE, smoked
  The Forsts
  McArthur's Smokehouse, Inc.
  Ozark Mountain Smoke House,
    Inc.
SAUSAGE, stick
  Amana Society
SAUSAGE, summer
  The Swiss Colony
SAUSAGE with sauerkraut
  Paprikas Weiss Importer

SAVORY
  Aphrodesia
  Paprikas Weiss Importer
  Rocky Hollow Herb Farm
  Roth and Son
SAW palmetto berries
  Aphrodesia
  Magic Garden Herb Co.
  Rocky Hollow Herb Farm
SCOTCH broom
  Magic Garden Herb Co.
SCOURING rush herb
  Roth and Son
SCUNGILLI
  Manganaro Foods
SEA cucumber
  Kam Shing Co.
SEA wrack
  Magic Garden Herb Co.
SEAFOOD, imported
  Breman House, Inc.
SEAFOOD seasoning
  Paprikas Weiss Importer
SEASONING (see also under
    type, e.g. Pizza seasoning,
    also under Spices/seasoners)
SEASONING, cracked pepper
  Paprikas Weiss Importer
SEASONING for snails
  Les Echalottes
SEASONING, roast meat
  Paprikas Weiss Importer
SEASONING salt
  Paprikas Weiss Importer
SEASONING, sauces
  Breman House, Inc.
  Charlotte Charles, Inc.

SEAWEED (see under specific
    type, e.g., Nori, Wakame,
    etc.)
SEAWEED, dried
  Kam Shing Co.
SELF-heal
  Old Town Natural Foods
SEMOLINA
  Paprikas Weiss Importer
  Sahadi Import Co.
SENBONZUKE
  Katagiri
SENCHA
  Katagiri
SENDAI
  Katagiri
SENGIRI daikon
  Katagiri
SENNA
  Roth and Son
SENNA leaves
  Aphrodesia
SENNA pods
  Aphrodesia
SESAME butter (see Butter,
    sesame)
SESAME paste
  Kam Shing Co.
  Oriental Country Store
SESAME seeds
  Aphrodesia
  Deer Valley Farm
  L. & L. Health Foods Co.
  Old Town Natural Foods
  Oriental Country Store
  Paprikas Weiss Importer
  Rocky Hollow Herb Farm

Roth and Son
SESAME tahini
  Aphrodesia
SHAD roe
  Les Echalottes
SHALLOTS
  Aphrodesia
  Les Echalottes
  Paprikas Weiss Importer
SHARK'S fin
  Kam Shing Co.
  Oriental Country Store
SHELL noodles
  Paprikas Weiss Importer
SHERRY cheese roll
  The Swiss Colony
SHERRY log roll
  The Swiss Colony
SHICHIMI togarashi
  Katagiri
SHINANO soba
  Katagiri
SHINSHU
  Katagiri
SHIOKOBU
  Katagiri
SHIO-endo
  Katagiri
SHIRATAMAKO
  Katagiri
SHISONAJIMI
  Katagiri
SHISONOMI-zuke
  Katagiri
SHITAKE (ashikiri)
  Katagiri
SHOGA-no-ko, powdered ginger
  Katagiri

SHOGA senbei
  Katagiri
SHOOTS, bamboo (see Bamboo
  shoots)
SHORTBREADS (see Biscuits,
  sweet/shortbreads)
SHRIMP/shrimp products
  Breman House, Inc.
  Charlotte Charles, Inc.
  Embassy Seafoods
  Omaha Steaks International
  Oriental Country Store
  R. H. Chamberlin
  Sahadi Import Co.
  Saltwater Farm
  Stock Yards Packing Co., Inc.
SHRIMP bisque
  Les Echalottes
SHRIMP chips
  Kam Shing Co.
  Oriental Country Store
SHRIMP wafers
  Les Echalottes
SILVER shots
  Paprikas Weiss Importer
  Roth and Son
SKULLCAP
  Aphrodesia
  The Herb Lady
  Lhasa Karnak Herb Co.
  Magic Garden Herb Co.
  Old Town Natural Foods
  Rocky Hollow Herb Farm
SLIPPERY elm
  Roth and Son
SLIPPERY elm bark
  Aphrodesia
  Old Town Natural Foods

Rocky Hollow Herb Farm
SLIPPERY elm candy (see Candy, slippery elm)
SLOE berries
Rocky Hollow Herb Farm
SMART weed
Magic Garden Herb Co.
SMITHFIELD ham, bacon (see Ham, Smithfield and Bacon, Smithfield)
SMOKEE triangles
The Swiss Colony
SNAIL gift set
Manganaro Foods
SNAILS (see also Escargots)
Charlotte Charles, Inc.
SNAPPER, red
R. H. Chamberlin
Omaha Steaks International
Saltwater Farm
SNOW peas
Les Echalottes
SOAP root
Sahadi Import Co.
SOLOMON'S seal
Aphrodesia
SOMEN
Katagiri
SOPRESSATA
Manganaro Foods
SORREL
Les Echalottes
SOUFFLE, chocolate
Les Echalottes
SOUJOUK
Sahadi Import Co.
SOUP (see also Fruit soup mixes)

SOUP bags (flavoring)
Les Echalottes
SOUP, bean with potatoes
Les Echalottes
SOUP, beef
Deer Valley Farm
SOUP, bird's nest
Les Echalottes
SOUP, Chinese
Charlotte Charles, Inc.
SOUP, cream
Charlotte Charles, Inc.
SOUP, cream of vichyssoise
Les Echalottes
SOUP, fish
Paprikas Weiss Importer
SOUP, French
Charlotte Charles, Inc.
SOUP, French onion
Les Echalottes
SOUP, lentil
Sahadi Import Co.
SOUP, lentil with potatoes
Les Echalottes
SOUP, minestrone
Manganaro Foods
Sahadi Import Co.
SOUP mix, celery
Paprikas Weiss Importer
SOUP mix, chicken noodle
Paprikas Weiss Importer
SOUP mix, consomme celestine
Paprikas Weiss Importer
SOUP mix, egg shell noodle
Paprikas Weiss Importer
SOUP mix, green pea
Paprikas Weiss Importer

SOUP mix, Italian rice
  Paprikas Weiss Importer
SOUP mix, leek
  Paprikas Weiss Importer
SOUP mix, liver dumpling
  Paprikas Weiss Importer
SOUP mix, mushroom
  Paprikas Weiss Importer
SOUP mix, oxtail
  Paprikas Weiss Importer
SOUP mix, potato
  Paprikas Weiss Importer
SOUP mix, vermicelli
  Paprikas Weiss Importer
SOUP mix, vichysoisse
  Paprikas Weiss Importer
SOUP mixes
  Charlotte Charles, Inc.
SOUP, mock turtle
  Les Echalottes
SOUP, mushroom
  Les Echalottes
SOUP noodles
  Paprikas Weiss Importer
SOUP, oxtail
  Les Echalottes
SOUP, pea with potatoes
  Les Echalottes
SOUP, shark's fin
  Les Echalottes
SOUP, snail
  Les Echalottes
SOUP, tomato
  Les Echalottes

SOUP, turtle
  Charlotte Charles, Inc.
  Les Echalottes
SOUP, vegetable
  Deer Valley Farm
SOUP, watercress
  Les Echalottes
SOUR cherry flavoring (see
    Flavoring, sour cherry)
SOUR drops
  Roth and Son
SOUR fruit slices
  Paprikas Weiss Importer
SOUR salt
  Aphrodesia
  Paprikas Weiss Importer
  Roth and Son
SOURWOOD leaves
  Aphrodesia
SOUTHERN John the conqueror
    root
  Aphrodesia
SOUTHERNWOOD
  Aphrodesia
  Rocky Hollow Herb Farm
SOY bean curd
  Kam Shing Co.
SOY flour (see Flour, soy)
SOY sauce
  Kam Shing Co.
  Oriental Country Store
SOY sauce, Java
  Les Echalottes
SOY sauce, Kikoman
  Kam Shing Co.
SOY sauce, Tamari
  Chico-San, Inc.

Deer Valley Farm
SOYBEAN products
Deer Valley Farm
SOYBEANS
    Chico-San, Inc.
    Deer Valley Farm
    Jaffe Bros. Natural Foods
    L. & L. Health Foods Co.
    Old Town Natural Foods
    Paprikas Weiss Importer
    Rocky Hollow Herb Farm
SPAETZLE
    Roth and Son
SPAETZLE, egg, Swabian
    Paprikas Weiss Importer
SPAETZLE, German style
    Paprikas Weiss Importer
SPAETZLE, Maggi
    Paprikas Weiss Importer
SPAGHETTI sauce
    Deer Valley Farm
SPEARMINT
    Aphrodesia
    Lhasa Karnak Herb Co.
    Old Town Natural Foods
    Rocky Hollow Herb Farm
SPEARMINT leaves
    Roth and Son
SPEEDWELL herb
    Magic Garden Herb Co.
SPICE (see also Pickling spice,
    Seasoning, etc.)
SPICE bush berries
    Rocky Hollow Herb Farm
SPICE bush twigs
    Rocky Hollow Herb Farm
SPICE drops
    Roth and Son

SPICE for spice cake
    Paprikas Weiss Importer
SPICES
    Breman House, Inc.
    Roth and Son
SPICES/seasoners
    Shoffeitt Products Corp.
SPIKENARD
    Aphrodesia
    Magic Garden Herb Co.
    Old Town Natural Foods
SPORTSTIX
    The Swiss Colony
SPRATTS in oil
    Les Echalottes
SPREADS, Mexican (see Dips/
    spreads, Mexican)
SPRINKLES, chocolate
    Paprikas Weiss Importer
SQUASH
    Sahadi Import Co.
SQUAW weed
    Magic Garden Herb Co.
SQUID
    Charlotte Charles, Inc.
    Oriental Country Store
    Sahadi Import Co.
STAR anise
    Old Town Natural Foods
    Rocky Hollow Herb Farm
    Roth and Son
STARCH, oriental cooking
    Chico-San, Inc.
STEAK
    Bissinger's
STEAK and kidney pie
    Les Echalottes
    Paprikas Weiss Importer

STEAK and mushroom pie
  Les Echalottes
STEAK, filet mignon
  The Forsts
  Omaha Steaks International
  Saltwater Farm
  Stock Yards Packing Co., Inc.
  The Swiss Colony
STEAK, porterhouse
  Omaha Steaks International
STEAK, rib
  Omaha Steaks International
  Stock Yards Packing Co., Inc.
STEAK seasoning, garlic
  Paprikas Weiss Importer
STEAK, sirloin
  Omaha Steaks International
  Saltwater Farm
  Stock Yards Packing Co., Inc.
STEAK, strip
  The Forsts
  Omaha Steaks International
  The Swiss Colony
STEAK, T-bone
  Omaha Steaks International
  Stock Yards Packing Co., Inc.
STEAK, tenderloin
  The Swiss Colony
STILLINGIA root
  Rocky Hollow Herb Farm
STOLLEN (see Christmas butter)
STONE root
  Magic Garden Herb Co.
STORAGE foods (see Camping/
    storage foods)
STRASBOURG pate (see Pates)

STRAWBERRIES, wild, in syrup
  Paprikas Weiss Importer
STRAWBERRY buds
  The Swiss Colony
STRAWBERRY leaves
  Aphrodesia
  Magic Garden Herb Co.
  Rocky Hollow Herb Farm
  The Swiss Colony
STRAWBERRY nut torte
  The Swiss Colony
STRUDEL flour
  Roth and Son
STUFFED vine leaves
  Les Echalottes
  Paprikas Weiss Importer
  Sahadi Import Co.
STOMACH bitters
  Paprikas Weiss Importer
STURGEON, smoked
  Les Echalottes
SUBGUM, sweet
  Kam Shing Co.
SUGAR, brown
  Deer Valley Farm
SUGAR, date
  Deer Valley Farm
SUGAR shots, colored
  Paprikas Weiss Importer
SUKIMIDARI
  Katagiri
SUKIYAKI furikake
  Katagiri
SUKONBU
  Katagiri
SUMAC
  Aphrodesia

Roth and Son
Sahadi Import Co.
SUMAC berries
Rocky Hollow Herb Farm
SUMMER savory
Paprikas Weiss Importer
SUNFLOWER seeds
Charlotte Charles, Inc.
Deer Valley Farm
L. & L. Health Foods Co.
Old Town Natural Foods
Rocky Hollow Herb Farm
Roth and Son
Sahadi Import Co.
Victoria Packing Corp.
SUNFLOWERS
Aphrodesia
SUPARE (mangalore)
Aphrodesia
SURUME
Katagiri
SUSHISU (mitsukan)
Katagiri
SUZUKI
Katagiri
SUZUKO kasuzuke
Katagiri
SWEET potatoes/yams
Charlotte Charles, Inc.
SWEET root
Roth and Son
SWISS chocolate (see Chocolate, Swiss)
SWISS fondue
Les Echalottes
SWISS fondue, rarebit
Les Echalottes

SYRUP, almond (see also Syrup, orgeat)
Sahadi Import Co.
SYRUP, French
Manganaro Foods
SYRUP, Lyle's golden
Roth and Son
SYRUP, maple (see Maple syrup)
SYRUP, mint
Les Echalottes
SYRUP, Motta
Manganaro Foods
SYRUP, orgeat (almond)
Les Echalottes
SYRUP, pomegranate
Sahadi Import Co.
SYRUP, wild black currant
Paprikas Weiss Importer
SYRUP, wild elderberry
Paprikas Weiss Importer
SYRUP, wild fruit of rose
Paprikas Weiss Importer
SYRUP, wild gooseberry
Paprikas Weiss Importer
SYRUP, wild raspberry
Paprikas Weiss Importer
SYRUP, wild red currant
Paprikas Weiss Importer
SYRUP, wild sour cherry
Paprikas Weiss Importer
SYRUP, wild strawberry
Paprikas Weiss Importer
SYRUPS, fruit
Breman House, Inc.
Charlotte Charles, Inc.
Deer Valley Farm

SYRUPS, grain
   Chico-San, Inc.
   Deer Valley Farm
SYRUPS, Swiss
   Paprikas Weiss Importer
TACO sauce
   Les Echalottes
TAG alder bark
   Aphrodesia
TAHINI (see Sesame, tahini)
TAMALES
   Charlotte Charles, Inc.
TAMARIND
   Aphrodesia
   Roth and Son
   Sahadi Import Co.
TANGELOS
   R. H. Chamberlin
   Lee's Fruit Co., Inc.
   Pavone Ranch
   The Swiss Colony
TANGERINE peel
   Aphrodesia
TANGERINES
   Pavone Ranch
TANSY
   Aphrodesia
   Old Town Natural Foods
   Rocky Hollow Herb Farm
TAPIOCA
   Les Echalottes
   Roth and Son
TAPIOCA, pearl
   Paprikas Weiss Importer
TARAKO shiozuke
   Katagiri
TARAMA, fish roe
   Sahadi Import Co.

TARRAGON
   Aphrodesia
   Deer Valley Farm
   Magic Garden Herb Co.
   Paprikas Weiss Importer
ROCKY
   Rocky Hollow Herb Farm
   Roth and Son
TARRAGON leaves in vinegar —
   estragon
   Les Echalottes
TEA, abfuehr
   Roth and Son
TEA, arterien
   Roth and Son
TEA, asthma
   Roth and Son
TEA, baldrian
   Roth and Son
TEA, black
   Caravel Coffee Co.
   Empire Coffee and Tea Co
   Northwestern Coffee Mills
   Paprikas Weiss Importer
TEA, blends
   Caravel Coffee Co.
   Empire Coffee and Tea Co
   Grace Tea Co., Ltd.
   The Herb Lady
   Lhasa Karnak Herb Co.
   Northwestern Coffee Mills
   Rocky Hollow Herb Farm
   Schapira Coffee Co.
TEA, blutreinigung
   Roth and Son
TEA, boemboe gulai
   Roth and Son

TEA, breast
  Paprikas Weiss Importer
  Roth and Son
TEA, centaury
  Roth and Son
TEA, Ceylon
  Empire Coffee and Tea Co.
  Grace Tea Co., Ltd.
  Northwestern Coffee Mills
  Schapira Coffee Co.
  The Swiss Colony
TEA, Ceylon breakfast
  Les Echalottes
  Paprikas Weiss Importer
TEA, cha ching
  The Swiss Colony
TEA, chamomile
  Manganaro Foods
TEA, chamomile, Hungarian
  Paprikas Weiss Importer
TEA, China black
  Paprikas Weiss Importer
TEA, Chinese People's Republic
  Empire Coffee and Tea Co.
TEA, Chinese restaurant
  Paprikas Weiss Importer
TEA, chunmee green
  Paprikas Weiss Importer
TEA, colonial
  Rocky Hollow Herb Farm
TEA, daon salam
  Roth and Son
TEA, daon sereh
  Roth and Son
TEA, darjeeling
  Caravel Coffee Co.
  Empire Coffee and Tea Co.
  Grace Tea Co., Ltd.

  Les Echalottes
  Northwestern Coffee Mills
  Paprikas Weiss Importer
  Roth and Son
  Schapira Coffee Co.
TEA, diet
  Roth and Son
TEA, djerek
  Roth and Son
TEA, Earl Grey
  Les Echalottes
  Empire Coffee and Tea Co.
  Grace Tea Co., Ltd.
  Northwestern Coffee Mills
  Paprikas Weiss Importer
  Roth and Son
  Schapira Coffee Co.
TEA, English
  Breman House, Inc.
  Charlotte Charles, Inc.
  Empire Coffee and Tea Co.
  Grace Tea Co., Ltd.
  Northwestern Coffee Mills
  The Swiss Colony
TEA, English breakfast
  Les Echalottes
  Paprikas Weiss Importer
  Roth and Son
TEA, eyebright
  Roth and Son
TEA, flatulenz
  Roth and Son
TEA, Formosa
  Charlotte Charles, Inc.
  Empire Coffee and Tea Co.
  Grace Tea Co., Ltd.
  Northwestern Coffee Mills
  Schapira Coffee Co.

TEA, Formosa oolong
  Les Echalottes
  Paprikas Weiss Importer
  Roth and Son
  Schapira Coffee Co.
TEA, galle/leber
  Roth and Son
TEA, German mint
  Paprikas Weiss Importer
TEA, green
  Caravel Coffee Co.
  Empire Coffee and Tea Co
  Northwestern Coffee Mills
  Old Town Natural Foods
  Schapira Coffee Co.
TEA, gun powder
  Roth and Son
TEA, haemorhoide
  Roth and Son
TEA, herb
  Breman House, Inc.
  Celestial Seasonings
  Chico-San, Inc.
  Deer Valley Farm
TEA, herz
  Roth and Son
TEA, husten
  Roth and Son
TEA, Irish
  Empire Coffee and Tea Co.
TEA, Irish breakfast
  Les Echalottes
  Paprikas Weiss Importer
TEA, jasmine
  Empire Coffee and Tea Co.
  Grace Tea Co., Ltd.
  Les Echalottes

Northwestern Coffee Mills
Paprikas Weiss Importer
Roth and Son
Schapira Coffee Co.
The Swiss Colony
TEA, kamillen
  Roth and Son
TEA, Keemun black
  Paprikas Weiss Importer
TEA, Keemun China
  Les Echalottes
TEA, kentjur
  Roth and Son
TEA, kieselsaeure
  Roth and Son
TEA, Laos
  Roth and Son
TEA, lapsang souchong
  Les Echalottes
  Empire Coffee and Tea Co.
  Grace Tea Co., Ltd.
  Northwestern Coffee Mills
  Paprikas Weiss Importer
  Roth and Son
  Schapira Coffee Co.
TEA, linden
  Aphrodesia
  Roth and Son
TEA, lung ching green dragon
  Paprikas Weiss Importer
TEA, magen
  Roth and Son
TEA, mandarin
  The Swiss Colony
TEA, mimosa oolong
  Paprikas Weiss Importer
TEA, ming cha
  Roth and Son

TEA, mint
  De Sousa's—The Healthians
  Empire Coffee and Tea Co.
  The Swiss Colony
TEA, Morman
  Magic Garden Herb Co.

TEA, mu
  Aphrodesia
  Old Town Natural Foods
TEA, nerven
  Roth and Son
TEA, oolong
  Empire Coffee and Tea Co.
  Grace Tea Co., Ltd.
  Northwestern Coffee Mills
  Paprikas Weiss Importer
  Schapira Coffee Co.
TEA, orange pekoe
  Empire Coffee and Tea Co.
  Les Echalottes
  Paprikas Weiss Importer
TEA, orange spice
  Paprikas Weiss Importer
TEA, panfried green
  Roth and Son
TEA, Paraguay
  Aphrodesia
TEA, peppermint
  Roth and Son
TEA, Prince of Wales
  Les Echalottes
TEA, poeroet
  Roth and Son
TEA, Queen Mary's
  Les Echalottes
TEA, raspberry leaf
  Roth and Son

TEA, rheuma
  Roth and Son
TEA, Russian samovar
  Paprikas Weiss Importer
TEA, sassafras
  Paprikas Weiss Importer
TEA, spearmint
  Paprikas Weiss Importer
TEA, Taiwan keemun
  Roth and Son
TEA, trappers
  Rocky Hollow Herb Farm
TEA, valley
  Rocky Hollow Herb Farm
TEA, verbena
  Empire Coffee and Tea Co.
TEA, yingteh black
  Paprikas Weiss Importer
TEA, zen green
  Paprikas Weiss Importer
TECRINE bordelaise
  Paprikas Weiss Importer
TEMPURA mix
  Katagiri
TEMPURA sauce (base)
  Katagiri
TEMPURAKO
  Katagiri
TERIYAKI sauce
  Katagiri
TERRINE bordelaise au vin de
      sauternes
  Les Echalottes
THYME
  Aphrodesia
  Deer Valley Farm
  Lhasa Karnak Herb Co.
  Magic Garden Herb Co.

Paprikas Weiss Importer
Rocky Hollow Herb Farm
Roth and Son
TIGER balm
Aphrodesia
TILIA flowers
Paprikas Weiss Importer
TOASTS/crispbreads
Charlotte Charles, Inc.
Deer Valley Farm
TOFFEE, butter
The Swiss Colony
TOFFEES
Charlotte Charles, Inc.
The Swiss Colony
TOMATOES
The Appleyard Corporation
Charlotte Charles, Inc.
Deer Valley Farm
Manganaro Foods
TOMATOES, risotto
Manganaro Foods
TONICS
Breman House, Inc.
TOOR dall
Sahadi Import Co.
TOROROKOBU
Katagiri
TORRONE
Manganaro Foods
TORTE (see also under specific
type, e.g., Linzer torte, etc.)
TORTE, butter creme
TORTILLAS, canned
Les Echalottes
TRAGACANTHE gum
Aphrodesia

TRIGONA
Sahadi Import Co.
TRIPES
Les Echalottes
Manganaro Foods
Paprikas Weiss Importer
TROUT, smoked
McArthur's Smokehouse, Inc.
TRUFFLES
Les Echalottes
Manganaro Foods
Paprikas Weiss Importer
Roth and Son
Sahadi Import Co.
TRUFFLES, black
Manganaro Foods
TRUFFLES, white
Sahadi Import Co.
TSUJUIRA (fortune) senbei
Katagiri
TSUKUDANI
Katagiri
TSUYU-no-moto (ninben)
Katagiri
TUNA
Charlotte Charles, Inc.
Embassy Seafoods
Manganaro Foods
TUNA filets
Les Echalottes
Manganaro Foods
TUNA, French
Manganaro Foods
TURKEY, barbeque
Smithfield Ham and Products
Co., Inc.
TURKEY, mixed dark and white
Les Echalottes

TURKEY, smoked
  The Forsts
  Omaha Steaks International
  Ozark Mountain Smoke House,
    Inc.
  The Swiss Colony
TURKISH chiveci
  Paprikas Weiss Importer
TURKISH delight
  Paprikas Weiss Importer
  Sahadi Import Co.
TURKISH delight, pistachio filled
  Sahadi Import Co.
TURKISH halawa (see Halawa,
    Turkish)
TURKISH leek
  Sahadi Import Co.
TURMERIC
  Aphrodesia
  Lhasa Karnak Herb Co.
  Paprikas Weiss Importer
  Rocky Hollow Herb Farm
  Roth and Son
  Sahadi Import Co.
TURNIPS, pickled
  Sahadi Import Co.
TURTLE seasoning
  Roth and Son
UDON kaku (shimodaya)
  Katagiri
UME amazuke
  Katagiri
UME kobucha
  Katagiri
UMEBOSHI
  Katagiri

UMEBOSHI chazuke
  Katagiri
UNINERI
  Katagiri
URAD dall
  Sahadi Import Co.
URBANI truffles
  Les Echalottes
UVA ursi
  Aphrodesia
  Old Town Natural Foods
  Rocky Hollow Herb Farm
UVA ursi leaves
  Lhasa Karnal Herb Co.
VALERIAN root
  Aphrodesia
  The Herb Lady
  Lhasa Karnak Herb Co.
  Magic Garden Herb Co.
  Old Town Natural Foods
  Paprikas Weiss Importer
  Rocky Hollow Herb Farm
  Roth and Son
VANILLA beans
  Aphrodesia
  Paprikas Weiss Importer
  Rocky Hollow Herb Farm
  Roth and Son
VANILLA flavoring
  Paprikas Weiss Importer
VANILLA pecan logs
  The Swiss Colony
VANILLA souffle
  Les Echalottes
VANILLIN
  Aphrodesia

VANILLIN powder
  Sahadi Import Co.
VANILLIN sugar
  Paprikas Weiss Importer
VARIAN
  Kalustyan
VEAL
  Omaha Steaks International
  Stock Yards Packing Co., Inc.
VEAL, quenelles of, naturel
  Les Echalottes
VEAL, quenelles of, with
      mushroom sauce
  Les Echalottes
VEGETABLE flakes
  Aphrodesia
VEGETABLE jardiniere
  Manganaro Foods
VEGETABLES, imported
  Breman House, Inc.
VEGETABLES, mixed
  Manganaro Foods
  Sahadi Import Co.
VEGETABLES, sea
  Chico-San, Inc.
  Deer Valley Farm
VEGETARIAN meat substitutes
  Newfoundland Book and Bible
  House
VENISON casserole
  Les Echalottes
VENISON filets
  Paprikas Weiss Importer
VENISON with mushrooms
  Paprikas Weiss Importer
VENTRASCA
  Manganaro Foods

VERBENA, lemon
  Aphrodesia
  Magic Garden Herb Co.
  Old Town Natural Foods
  Rocky Hollow Herb Farm
  Roth and Son
VERMICELLI
  Sahadi Import Co.
VERVAIN
  Aphrodesia
  Lhasa Karnak Herb Co.
  Rocky Hollow Herb Farm
VERVAIN, blue
  Old Town Natural Foods
VETIVERT
  Aphrodesia
VIENNA neapolitans
  Paprikas Weiss Importer
VIENNESE lady fingers
  Paprikas Weiss Importer
VINEGAR
  Charlotte Charles, Inc.
  Chico-San, Inc.
  Deer Valley Farm
  Victoria Packing Corp.
VINEGAR, black
  Kam Shing Co.
VINEGAR, French
  Manganaro Foods
VINEGAR, Italian
  Manganaro Foods
VINEGAR, rose wine
  Les Echalottes
VINEGAR, sauterne domestic
  Manganaro Foods
VINEGAR, tarragon
  Les Echalottes

VINEGAR, wine
  Sahadi Import Co.
VIOLET leaves
  Aphrodesia
  Old Town Natural Foods
VIOLETS, crystallized
  Aphrodesia
VITAMINS (see Food
  supplements/ vitamins)
WAFER papers
  Paprikas Weiss Importer
WAFERS, French
  Les Echalottes
WAFERS, India
  Paprikas Weiss Importer
WAFER sheets, pischinger style
  Roth and Son
WAHOO bark
  Aphrodesia
WAKAME
  Katagiri
WALNUT leaves
  Aphrodesia
  Lhasa Karnak Herb Co.
  Paprikas Weiss Importer
WALNUTS
  Jaffe Bros. Natural Foods
  L. & L. Health Foods Co.
  Paprikas Weiss Importer
  Rocky Hollow Herb Farm
WALNUTS, English
  The Swiss Colony
WALNUTS, pickled
  Les Echalottes
  Paprikas Weiss Importer
WALNUTS, shelled
  Sahadi Import Co.

WASABIKO
  Katagiri
WATER chestnut
  Kam Shing Co.
  Les Echalottes
  Oriental Country Store
WATER eryngo root
  Aphrodesia
WATER pepper
  Aphrodesia
WATERMELON
  Lee's Fruit Co., Inc.
WATERMELON seeds
  Aphrodesia
WAX (see Bees wax)
WHEAT for soup
  Roth and Son
WHEAT germ
  Deer Valley Farm
  L. &.L. Health Foods Co.
  Paprikas Weiss Importer
  Rocky Hollow Herb Farm
  Roth and Son
WHEAT, hulled
  Roth and Son
WHEAT pilaf
  Les Echalottes
  Paprikas Weiss Importer
  Roth and Son
  Sahadi Import Co.
WHEAT, shelled
  Sahadi Import Co.
WHEY/whey products
  Deer Valley Farm
WHITE ash bark
  Aphrodesia
WHITE ice cap chocolate
  Paprikas Weiss Importer

WHITE oak bark
  Aphrodesia
  Magic Garden Herb Co.
  Old Town Natural Foods
WHITE oblatten
  Roth and Son
WHITE pine bark
  Old Town Natural Foods
WHITE willow bark
  Aphrodesia
WHOLE wheat berries
  Jaffe Bros. Natural Foods]
  Rocky Hollow Herb Farm
WHOLE wheat bread (see Bread,
  whole wheat)
WILD cherry bark
  Aphrodesia
  Old Town Natural Foods
WILD yam root
  Aphrodesia
WILLOW bark, black
  Aphrodesia
WINE making supplies (see Beer/
  wine making supplies)
WINTERGREEN
  Aphrodesia
  Old Town Natural Foods
WITCH grass
  Magic Garden Herb Co.
WITCH hazel
  Aphrodesia
  Old Town Natural Foods
WITCH hazel bark
  Rocky Hollow Herb Farm
WOOD betony
  Aphrodesia
  Magic Garden Herb Co.

WOODRUFF
  Aphrodesia
  Paprikas Weiss Importer
  Rocky Hollow Herb Farm
  Roth and Son
WORMSEED
  Aphrodesia
WORMWOOD
  Magic Garden Herb Co.
  Rocky Hollow Herb Farm
WORMWOOD, Roman
  Rocky Hollow Herb Farm
WURST (see Sausage)
YACHIYO fa
  Katagiri
YAKI ika ajitsuke
  Katagiri
YAKINORI sushimaki
  Katagiri
YAMAGATAYA sencha
  Katagiri
YAMAJIRUSHI
  Katagiri
YAMASA shimmi
  Katagiri
YAMASA shoyu
  Katagiri
YAMATOYAKI (shio senbei)
  Katagiri
YARROW
  Lhasa Karnak Herb Co.
  Old Town Natural Foods
  Roth and Son
YARROW flowers
  Rocky Hollow Herb Farm
YEAST (see Baking powders/
  yeast)

YELLOW dock
  Aphrodesia
  Rocky Hollow Herb Farm
YERBA mate
  Aphrodesia
  Rocky Hollow Herb Farm
  Roth and Son
YERBA santa
  Aphrodesia
  Rocky Hollow Herb Farm
YOGURT culture
  Daisyfresh Yogurt Co.
  Deer Valley Farm
YOHIMBE bark
  The Herb Lady
  Magic Garden Herb Co.
YOKAM
  Katagiri
YOSABUROZUKE
  Katagiri
YOSHINOKUZU
  Katagiri
YULE log
  The Swiss Colony
YULE wreath (see Chocolate
    yule wreath)
YUMA root
  Magic Garden Herb Co.
ZAATAR
  Sahadi Import Co.
ZAMPINO
  Manganaro Foods
ZENMAI
  Katagiri

OLIVER PRESS

Presents

the

Finder's
Guide
Series

KITS & PLANS

FINDER'S GUIDE No. 1

Joseph Rosenbloom

This book offers the do-it-yourselfer a complete directory of companies and equipment available for many diversified projects and plans. This indexed directory solves the problem of finding out "who" makes "what." There is something here for every taste and level of skill.

288 pp
LC 73-92459 $3.95

Kits and Plans for the Budget Minded

CRAFT SUPPLIES SUPERMARKET

FINDER'S GUIDE No. 2

Joseph Rosenbloom

A well illustrated and indexed directory of craft supplies. Thousands of products, including materials, kits, tools, etc., from over 450 companies, are analyzed from their catalogs.

224 pp, ill., August 1974
LC 74-84298 $3.95

THE COMPLETE KITCHEN

FINDER'S GUIDE No. 3

Anne Heck

This book is a comprehensive guide to hard-to-find utensils, and describes the companies supplying such utensils as well as giving information about their catalogs. Many illustrations of unusual or interesting utensils.

96 pp, ill., September, **1974**
LC 74-84299 $2.95

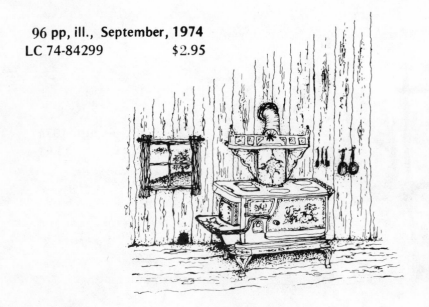

HOMEGROWN ENERGY

FINDER'S GUIDE No. 4

Power for the Home and Homestead

Gary Wade

This book offers the do-it-yourselfer a very complete directory to thousands of available products involved in the production of home grown power. Water wheels, solar cells, windmills, methane generators and other exotic equipment and parts are covered and indexed in depth.

96 pp, ill., September, 1974
LC 74-84300 $2.95

COUNTRY TOOLS

Essential Hardware and Livery

FINDER'S GUIDE No. 7

Fred Davis

Locates sources for the otherwise difficult to find tools essential to country living. This book covers everything from bell scrapers through goat harnesses to spoke shavers. An indispensible guide for the country resident working his land.

160pp, ill., February, 1975
$3.95

ᴛʜᴇ *Scribner Library*

America's Quality Paperback Series

CHARLES SCRIBNER'S SONS

Shipping and Billing Departments
Vreeland Ave., Totowa, New Jersey 07512

Order Blank

Dear Sirs:

I believe your new series "FINDER'S GUIDES" fills a
definite need for information and I would like to order:

QUANTITY	TITLE	TOTAL
	copies of KITS AND PLANS @ $3.95 ea.	
	copies of CRAFT SUPPLIES SUPERMARKET @ $3.95 ea.	
	copies of THE COMPLETE KITCHEN @ $2.95 ea.	
	copies of HOMEGROWN ENERGY @ $2.95 ea.	
	copies of SPICES, CONDIMENTS, TEAS, COFFEES, AND OTHER DELICACIES @ $3.95 ea.	
	copies of COUNTRY TOOLS @ $3.95 ea.	
	copies of ALL OF THE ABOVE BOOKS ($21.70 Total)	

NOTES

NOTES